W9-ARF-295

DISCARDED
JENKS LRC
GORDON COLLEGF

PROFESSIONAL DEVELOPMENT AND PRACTICE SERIES
Ann Lieberman, *Editor*

Editorial Advisory Board: Myrna Cooper, Nathalie Gehrke,
Gary Griffin, Judith Warren Little, Lynne Miller,
Phillip Schlechty, Gary Sykes

Building a Professional Culture in Schools
Ann Lieberman, Editor

The Contexts of Teaching in Secondary Schools: Teachers' Realities
Milbrey W. McLaughlin, Joan E. Talbert,
and Nina Bascia, Editors

Careers in the Classroom: When Teaching is More Than a Job
Sylvia Mei-Ling Yee

The Making of a Teacher: Teacher Knowledge and Teacher Education
Pamela L. Grossman

*Staff Development for Education in the 1990s:
New Demands, New Realities, New Perspectives*, SECOND EDITION
Ann Lieberman and Lynne Miller, Editors

*Teachers Who Lead: The Rhetoric of Reform and
the Realities of Practice*
Patricia A. Wasley

Exploring Teaching: Reinventing an Introductory Course
Sharon Feiman-Nemser and Helen J. Featherstone, Editors

Teaching: Making Sense of an Uncertain Craft
Joseph P. McDonald

TEACHING:
Making Sense
of an Uncertain Craft

Joseph P. McDonald

Teachers College, Columbia University
New York and London

JENKS L.R.C.
GORDON COLLEGE
255 GRAPEVINE RD.
WENHAM, MA 01984-1895

LB
1025.3
,M35
1992

Published by Teachers College Press, 1234 Amsterdam Avenue, New York, NY 10027

Copyright © 1992 Teachers College, Columbia University

All rights reserved. No part of this publication may be reproduced or transmitted in any form or by any means, electronic or mechanical, including photocopy, or any information storage and retrieval system, without permission from the publisher.

Library of Congress Cataloging-in-Publication Data
McDonald, Joseph P.
    Teaching : making sense of an uncertain craft / Joseph P. McDonald.
       p.   cm. — (Professional development and practice series)
    Includes bibliographical references (p.) and index.
    ISBN 0-8077-3168-4 (alk. paper). — ISBN 0-8077-3167-6 (pbk. : alk. paper)
    1. Teaching. 2. Education—United States—Aims and objectives.
I. Title. II. Series.
LB1025.3.M35   1992
371.1'02—dc20   91-44869

ISBN 0-8077-3167-6 (paper)
ISBN 0-8077-3168-4 (cloth)

Printed on acid-free paper
Manufactured in the United States of America

99 98 97 96 95 94 93 92   1 2 3 4 5 6 7 8

For the teachers in my family—past, present, and future:

especially Beth, Mary, Michael
and including John Moylan, who was exiled from
Ireland for teaching,
and his grandson, Si, my grandfather, who taught in a
one-room schoolhouse in the first decade of this
century.

Contents

Foreword, *by Ann Lieberman*   ix
Acknowledgments   xi

1   Uncertainty in Teaching   1
A Conspiracy of Certainty   2
Overturning the Conspiracy   6

2   Learning to Read Teaching   9
Perspectives from Practice   9
Theoretical Perspectives   15

3   Reading on the Trolley   20

4   Reading Over Pizza   42
Phases in the Group's Development   43
A Reading Experiment   45
Critical Reading   56

5   Reading in School   68
The Story: A Crisis of Incompletes   73
The Story, Closely Read   81

6   Reading for a Profession   101
Maggie Haley   105
Sylvia Ashton-Warner   111
Eliot Wigginton   115
An Uncertain Profession   122

Notes   125

References	129
Index	135
About the Author	145

Foreword

The purpose of the Professional Development and Practice Series is to present research, narratives, and description of cutting-edge work that leads to deeper understanding of educational practice and how to improve it. We are at a time of important educational change and especially need scholarship that illuminates the complexities of practice, helps us see old problems in new ways, and leads us to fresh insight. This volume definitely meets the need.

Teaching: Making Sense of an Uncertain Craft is a jewel of a book. It digs deeply into the tensions, contradictions, and uncertainties of teaching. It reveals images we work over, reflect upon, and finally tuck into our expanding repertoire of understandings about teaching. McDonald wants us to appreciate the uncertainties of teaching precisely because, if we do not, we will misunderstand how to move teachers to improve their practice.

His book brings us an authentic teacher's voice, then teaches us how to "read" it. This reading involves the application to practice and research of "simple if neglected things" like noticing, wondering, reflecting, and holding an impression in the grip of an idea. The lesson starts on the trolley, where we sit next to a teacher scribbling notes on his day in school. As he wonders what to do about two of his students, James and Shari, we see how conflict and caring co-exist. Reading his journal provides us a glimpse of the struggles seldom examined in other writing about teaching. We wonder along with him why teaching feels so precarious.

The reading lesson next proceeds to a description of a study group and its progress in moving from reading others (Adler, Boyer, et al.) to reading its members' own knowledge of their craft, thus giving strength to their own voice and subsequent vision. "Uncertainty" in teaching then continues as the leitmotif in a description of a school struggling to reform itself "from the bottom up": As a consultant/storyteller, McDonald helps one school's teachers by giving voice to their work, their stories, and their struggle to change policies in light of nagging dilemmas that never seem to go away.

The book ends with reading "for a profession"—reading and learning about heroic figures in our profession who have written about the greater and lesser moments of their own lives as teachers. The book challenges the idea that teaching as a profession lacks a written record. We are enriched by reading the record left by Margaret Haley, a teacher unionist, Sylvia Ashton-Warner, an extraordinary teacher of the Maoris in New Zealand, and Eliot Wigginton, a remarkable teacher from Georgia whose students created *Foxfire,* a journal with a twenty-five-year history.

Throughout this volume, we learn to read teaching in the company of teachers, and under the guidance of an author who writes poignantly and sensitively about himself and our collective struggle to know more, to understand more, and to feel comfortable with uncertainty as a centerpiece of teaching.

Ann Lieberman
Series Editor

Acknowledgments

This book has an origin that may seem selfish: a decade-long effort to make sense of me as a teacher. The effort might have stayed private, and doubtlessly stunted, except that others took a surprising interest along the way. My students, for example, not only let me teach them and secretly reflect upon the process, but some of them, perhaps noticing my wonder, began to reflect themselves upon what I was doing. I came to understand that as co-constructors of my teaching, they got as much out of analyzing it as I did. One of my high school students told me suddenly one day—as if reporting a long and fruitful study—that she had discovered that I teach principally with my hands. She was delighted by my shocked recognition, a confirmation of her empirical skills. I was delighted, too, because her comment turned my wonder for the first time toward who I am when I teach. I thought of her some number of years later while looking at photos of a strange me teaching at a university in Eastern Europe. The photographer—another of my students—had clearly been amused and astonished by my hands.

Once, in the spring semester of 1988, I had the opportunity to devote a whole course I was teaching at Brown to the question of what makes teaching a craft. My students and I devised the image of teaching there that I present here in Chapter 1. It was the product of much reading, interviewing, writing—collaborative inquiries that we fed to a slowly growing model. When we unveiled a final iteration of the model on the last day of class, I remember standing at the front of the classroom, thinking: "now I will let them watch me with our model in mind"; and I felt their intellectual satisfaction in the watching. I think it was the first time I recognized that a self-centered move in teaching is not necessarily a selfish one.

When students watch their teachers, a bond sometimes forms in the watching whose power exceeds the grasp of normal measures of learning. In the first year of the inquiry that has become this book, I had an opportunity some afternoons to do my own watching as a student of two teachers, Sara Lawrence Lightfoot and David Cohen. This book owes much to both of them not only because then and in other years they explicitly encouraged my work, but also because of the bonds formed in this watching between my work and theirs.

I want to acknowledge here by name the colleagues who have lent their voices to this book, since in the book itself—in order to protect their privacy—I have changed their names (except when referring to their published writing). They comprise several groups. First, my teaching colleagues in high school: Manson Hall, Bert Hirtle, Mark Petricone, and Faith Waters. Next, my colleagues in the Secondary Study Group: Marshall Cohen, Abby Erdman, Paula Evans, Jay Featherstone, Kathy Kaditz, Margaret Metzger, Judi Sandler, Paul Stein, Don Thomas, and Gene Thompson-Grove. Next, my school-based and Brown-based colleagues in the Coalition of Essential Schools: Nick Amaral, Wendy Aronoff, Traci Bliss, Paula Evans, Paul Gounaris, Lee Hoisington, David Kobrin, Pat McQuillan, Albin Moser, Ronnie Rancourt, Kay Scheidler, Grace Taylor, Miriam Toloudis, Nancy Topalian, and John Zilboorg.

Readers of the manuscript in various stages have included Rod Blakeman, Joe Check, Helen Featherstone, Jay Featherstone, Gerry Grant, David Kobrin, Tom James, Rick Lear, Fred Lighthall, Beth McDonald, Pat McQuillan, Albin Moser, Ned Rossiter, Kay Scheidler, Ted Sizer, Gene Thompson-Grove, Marue Walizer, Pat Wasley, and Eliot Wigginton. I wish to acknowledge their thoughtful reading. I would also like to thank Rich Bourgon, Jean Carroll, and Ann Goebel, who helped with manuscript preparation.

Several people, already mentioned at various points above, deserve a special acknowledgment, since there would simply be no book without David Cohen, Paula Evans, Sara Lightfoot, and Ted Sizer. They contributed contexts, theories, support, and more. Nor would there be a book without Beth McDonald, who contributed hundreds of evenings of insight from her own experience of teaching and of reading teaching. And then there's Basil, who has taught me more than I've taught him.

Books take time to write, and this one got its time from the generous support of the Spencer Fellowship Program of the National Academy of Education. I especially want to thank three of that body's members—Pat Graham, Lee Shulman, and Elliot Eisner. Finally, I want to thank Ann Lieberman for her timely support.

TEACHING:
Making Sense
of an Uncertain Craft

1

Uncertainty in Teaching

As soon as I finished teaching the first class I ever taught, I asked my supervisor what he thought. He told me he thought I had taught as if speaking from the next room through a tube. He was a good coach. With a single sentence, he oriented me toward the real thing. Whatever you do as you struggle to teach, he seemed to suggest, do it in person with kids you dare to be among, and keep all relations live.

Real teaching, I learned in time, happens inside a wild triangle of relations—among teacher, students, subject—and the points of this triangle shift continuously. What shall I teach amid all that I might teach? How can I grasp it myself so that my grasping may enable theirs? What are they thinking and feeling—toward me, toward each other, toward the thing I am trying to teach? How near should I come, how far off should I stay? How much clutch, how much gas?

Inside the triangle, clear evidence is very rare. Snarls and smiles mix disconcertingly. Right answers fade to wrong, and vice versa: a matter of interpretation, of how one construes a gesture or an attitude, of whether one thinks the moment demands more criticism or more encouragement, of how much energy one has to believe in teaching's effectiveness.

Yet out of the uncertainty, craft emerges. The wildness of the triangle provokes it. Although I never learn exactly where to stand in relation to my students, I develop a reliable sense of what is too close and what is too far. Within these limits, I craft a workable relationship for the moment—now here, now there. I tune my stance continually to the values that seize me. Similarly, though I remain chronically unsure of what to teach and how to teach it, I develop an eye for productive linkage. A corner of a text, perhaps, strikes me suddenly as offering the power to link me, them, and something worth knowing in the world. The link will be fundamentally intellectual, but it may seem almost physical when I spy it. I may trace its shape with my fingers as

1

if I had found a thing in the dark. But this is only a metaphor of reassurance: I can never be sure of the moves I must continually dare to make; the relations of teaching remain always skittish.

So I brace myself against pervasive doubts with bits of self, crafted from values: a confident idea, a resolute intention, an enthusiastic tone, an attention-gathering glance. I temporarily repress uncertainty in a believing persona. The teacher must keep casting, James Herndon (1985) says in a fly-fishing metaphor for teaching, *believing* in secret striped bass even when, on many occasions, there are none in the channel. Courageous believing knits up the relations of teaching: believing in some piece of meaning, believing in some kid's capacity to grasp it, believing that the grasp happens.

A CONSPIRACY OF CERTAINTY

Most people think, however, that teaching is much simpler than this. For instance, hardly anyone concerned with teaching—children, parents, school authorities, researchers, even teachers themselves—sees what I call the relation of the teacher to the subject as problematic.[1] What to teach is usually considered more or less a given. The teacher who wonders about it nonetheless is presumed to be wondering whether one set of givens is an appropriate match for another: Shall I teach the binomial theorem to *this* group? Hardly anyone worries about what I believe to be prior questions: Shall I invest *myself* in the binomial theorem? And if so, how? Similarly, the relation between teacher and students is generally presumed to be far more amenable to stable management than in my image of it: a matter of good "control" plus skillfulness in the use of motivational tools. Finally, what I regard as an exceedingly unpredictable relation between students and subject is rarely even thought to exist. In place of the active mutuality of a relation, people often imagine empty slots in kids' heads and ready-made data to put there. They overlook the fact that the most important things to learn continuously change shape, while minds continuously impose their own designs.[2]

Chief among the conspirators of certainty are the entrepreneurs of school improvement. They sit at the intersection of research, policy, and practice, where they proclaim bright ideas. The problem is that the bright ideas are often fixed ones. Just teach *what* we say and *as* we say, argue these entrepreneurs, and all the ambiguities of your worklife will disappear like so many vapors clouding up the real thing. But this is exactly the problem, John Dewey (1929) would say: Such a sense of the real thing is retrospective rather than prospective; it implicitly takes the messiness of actual teaching to be the margin of error in striving to fit a pattern, rather than the sign of freshness and uniqueness in a struggle to make the future. So bright ideas come and bright ideas go, and teachers lose track of their own craft in margins of error.

Teacher educators often join the conspiracy of certainty, too, by promoting sanitized images of teaching. They coach novices through the novices' first encounters with uncertainty—that monster which perches above a brand-new plan book and screams: "What will you teach, and what difference will it make?" Confronting the monster and learning to struggle with it respectfully are crucial steps in acquiring craft. Yet teacher educators often urge their charges instead to placate the monster with donations of certainty—Q: What will you teach? A: What I learned myself in school. Q: What difference will it make? A: That is indicated in these behavioral objectives, this curriculum guide backed by research.

Many researchers are conspirators, too, especially when the research they conduct fails to see beyond its own a priori assumptions. Once a researcher told me that he had given up school-based research since he had not been able to find a single school that matched his theoretical model of a just community. He was not inclined to adjust the model to what he had been able to find. Instead, he explored applications of the model in other settings and railed against the irrationality of schools. This is an extreme example, so the absurdity is easy to spot; but the conspiracy holds in subtler circumstances too. The reductive methods of much research—a striving to cut to what is considered to be the main point or the bottom line, whether in survey or case study—tend inadvertently to drain teaching of its unpredictabilities. And the discourse of research tends to flatten teaching's quirks. Reading it, the teacher may be sadly astonished at how much she has fretted over so little—how obviously, after all, one may distinguish between empowering and disparaging language, good and bad grouping practices, open or closed questions, and so forth. Some researchers, moreover, are notorious for assuming the entire role of knowledge creator, leaving no part of it for teachers—cheating teachers of their chance to know the messy side of theoretical development, cheating themselves of acquaintance with practical knowledge. Recently I read a particular researcher's list of questions "we still have not figured out" with regard to teaching. Its *we* was clearly exclusive of teachers, since the questions were entirely ones that teachers answer every teaching day simply because they have to—questions like how kids' thinking in school is affected by the backgrounds they bring to school, and what teachers can do about that; or how teachers can best combine caring for kids with teaching them how to think. From this researcher's tacit point of view, the answers that teachers continuously construct for such questions are inadequate because they are provisional rather than certain.[3]

Then there are the policy makers. On all levels, they tend to cut policies that are too stark, and frequently promote images of teaching that are too fixed. This is ironic, since the work of enacting policy is, in its messiness, very like the work of teaching.

> William J. Bennett, the nation's drug policy director, raised questions today about the effectiveness of drug education programs and said children were more likely to respond to aggressive law enforcement and assured punishment. In testimony before the Senate Judiciary Committee, Mr. Bennett rejected the argument espoused by leading Democrats and many outside experts that education was the major solution to the nation's drug problem. He offered an unsparing portrait of young drug abusers as knowing users, not innocent victims.
> . . . Senator Edward M. Kennedy, Democrat of Massachusetts, one of several committee members who challenged Mr. Bennett's position, said, "I continue to be deeply concerned that the administration underestimates the importance of treatment and education. We know that education can inoculate children against drug abuse." (Berke, 1990, p. 1)

Choose your favorite image of teaching from this front-page story in *The New York Times*. Bennett, the former Secretary of Education, portrays education as capable only of informing children, not of affecting their values or their sense of themselves. And Kennedy, Chairman of the Senate's Labor and Human Resources Committee that oversees education, portrays it as a form of inoculation. Neither image seems to me very suited to the formulation of policies respectful of teaching as it really is: capable in fact of transforming children's lives by helping them to save themselves from despair; equally capable of utterly failing in this effort despite all money, brilliance, and caring.

Again, this may be an extreme example, as well as one unlikely to have much of a practical impact—a rhetorical exchange only. But equally simplistic, if somewhat subtler, assumptions often get beyond the rhetorical stage in Washington and other policy centers. Occasionally, they have a massive influence. Consider, for example, a key assumption contained in the 1975 federal law, the Education for All Handicapped Children Act (P. L. 94-142). Inspired partly by civil rights legislation, the law capped a decade-long effort within the federal government to end a great injustice of American schooling (Singer & Butler, 1987). Before its implementation, beginning in 1977, children in many states were routinely denied public schooling because they were inconvenient to teach—needing special attention and support, needing unusual services or structures, perhaps requiring wheelchair access. Meanwhile, masses of other children were mislabeled, mistreated, and often stuck in dead-end basement classrooms.

The law introduced several entitlements and mechanisms that in fifteen years have transformed special education. It entitles all handicapped children to a free and public education—no more exclusions. It entitles them to obtain this education, moreover, in the least restrictive environment appropriate to their handicap. It guarantees parents the right to challenge the appropriateness of placements and otherwise to participate in important decisions involving special services for their children. Finally, the law mandates the individualized educational plan (IEP) as the documentary basis of special education. The IEP is to be the focus of school-parent negotiation, the ground upon which monitoring and evaluation proceed, and the teacher's prescription for teaching. It is the last of these three functions that is suspect in my view.[4] In fact, the kind of teaching the law means to foster is often called diagnostic-prescriptive teaching. The medical analogy implicit in the term goes beyond an association of handicapped children with medical services. It speaks to a yearning that permeates federal and state regulations in special education, and indeed in other areas, too (Wise, 1979). This is the yearning to make teaching more rational—the quest for certainty. Teachers should work as we like to think doctors do: Figure out what's wrong, then fix it.

The logic of the assertion seems compelling, but only outside the swirl of actual practice. The problem with IEPs is that they tend to overspecify. Although they have heuristic value, they do not make teaching more rational as it was hoped they would. They often hyperrationalize it instead (Wise, 1979). One consequence is that they become a burden on teaching and learning, a massive paperwork appendage that seldom directly helps kids and may indirectly hurt them by taking up their teacher's time.

Meanwhile, they—along with other artifacts of policy on all levels, and research-to-practice initiatives, and the lingering impact of their own education—infect teachers themselves with an inappropriate sense of certainty about their work. So teachers themselves become unwitting conspirators of certainty, even while they live with uncertainty day to day. The catalyst of their involvement in the conspiracy is a key feature of teaching mentioned above: Whenever they teach, teachers must to some extent swallow the uncertainty they feel, believe wholeheartedly in their goals and efforts, even though riddled by doubt. Otherwise, the class fails to move and may fall apart for lack of trust in the leader: Who is he to tell me what to do, when he doesn't even believe in himself? The most clear-sighted teachers manage simultaneously to reveal to their students—and to bear stolidly in mind themselves—that confidence and certainty are not the same thing and that doubt is a key intellectual tool. Still, the evidence of the others, and indeed of the entire institutional structure of schooling, is a powerful counterweight. After a while, everything can seem so given in school: that history and English are different subjects, that the third grade is when you teach cursive writing, that some students are "gifted" and others "special," and so on.

OVERTURNING THE CONSPIRACY

Why do I try to dispute such powerful influences? What is to be gained by insisting on a view of teaching as an uncertain craft? My answer, baldly put, is that if we could rout the idea that teaching is only about skill and method, if we could foster a public perception of its moral complexity, if we could honor the role played in teaching by the teacher's productively ambivalent self, then I think we would have a chance to build the kind of schools our children and grandchildren will need in the twenty-first century. These would be schools free of cultural smugness and of factory attitudes, where students and teachers were encouraged to engage genuinely in the messy and uncertain business of thinking, collaborating, and creating.

Today we are awash in reform initiatives that seek by various means to secure a better educational future. Many of these initiatives are well aimed, though destined for the doom that Cuban (1990) describes:

> Many reforms seldom go beyond getting adopted as a policy. Most get implemented in word rather than deed, especially in classrooms. What often ends up in districts and schools are signs of reform in new rules, different tests, revised organizational charts, and new equipment. Seldom are the deepest structures of schooling that are embedded in the school's use of time and space, teaching practices, and classroom routines fundamentally altered even at those historical moments when reforms seek those alterations as the goal. (p. 9)

I think this is because so many reform initiatives fail to acknowledge the uncertainty of teaching. In this respect, their champions may be gripped by a deep reluctance, widely shared, to admit uncertainty where such precious things are at stake: children, their future, our deepest values, our sense of what we know and of what we have achieved.

I dare to offer a different message only because I trust that when one opens oneself to the real complexities and uncertainties of life—even in precious realms—one gains not only a better understanding of life but also more grace and inventiveness in living. This is a paradox crucial to this book. In trying throughout its pages to unsettle ideas of certainty in teaching, I do not mean to cheat teaching of its hopes and intentionality, nor to invalidate society's right to expect teachers to be accountable for the effects of their work. In fact, I intend an exactly contrary effect.

I believe that an acknowledgment of fundamental uncertainty can enhance practical confidence and directedness, foster productivity and accountability, even raise hopes. In 1926, Werner Heisenberg showed that the more accurately one tries to measure the position of a particle, the less accurately one measures its speed, and that the resulting margin of uncertainty is a fundamental and inescapable feature of the world. But his insight did not hurt physics; it cut physics loose from the determinism that had enmeshed it since Newton. Physicists simply changed their search for immutable laws to a search for formulas that predict phenomena within specified levels of probability. They gave up certainty for a practical directedness more open to actual experience, and they were better off for it (Hawking, 1988). As Dewey claimed at about the same time (1929), uncertainty saves a place for novelty and genuine growth and change. When we accept uncertainty, he said, we transform our relationship to practical problems. They become the means by which we may see beyond what we think we know.

Such a transformation in our relationship to the practical problems of teaching could enhance our chances to improve teaching. This is because it would rid us of the burden of regarding teaching as perfectible. So long as Mrs. Zajac, whose teaching was chronicled by Kidder (1989), is surrounded by people who claim to know the perfect pattern for her teaching—what she should know about science, how she should group her fifth graders, how she should speak to them, and so on—she will want to keep her door closed. Many of these people have good ideas, but their ideas often form a pattern that

they would like Zajac to adopt wholesale, no questions asked. They
do not want to feed her craft; they want to dictate her practice. Their
urgency and her probable fear of it are both responses to a prevailing
ideology of teaching that regards it as liable to exacting judgment—
here it is done well, there it is done poorly. As ideologies will, this one
operates below the surface of our consciousness much of the time,
covertly governing the judgments we make of ourselves and others as
teachers, affecting not only teaching but our thoughts and talk about
teaching, the education of teachers, and studies of teaching. It kills
our capacity to appreciate teaching's practical wisdom, shuts us off
from the serendipity of practical invention, and keeps teachers behind
closed doors. In my view, an honest accounting of the uncertainties in
the craft of teaching can help open those doors, encourage collegiality
and experimentation, and promote an ethos of continuous rather than
periodic or sporadic improvement.

So how might we come to see certainty as a greater risk than
uncertainty in thinking about teaching? How might reformers, policy
makers, researchers, teacher educators, parents, and especially teachers themselves develop a sense of teaching as the crafting of a response
to uncertainties that elude definitive settlement?

I suggest we start by attending carefully to what teachers say.
Teachers are, after all, closest to teaching. Although they are as
weighted as other interested parties by false certainties, they must also
manage the work day by day as it actually is. One consequence is that,
at least tacitly, they come to know teaching's uncertainty and how to
manage it. This knowledge embeds itself in what they say. That is why
this is a book of teachers' voices, beginning with my own small voice
in Chapter 3, ending with a century of great voices in Chapter 6.
Along the way is a chronicle about learning to read teaching in the
voices of teachers.

2

Learning to Read Teaching

PERSPECTIVES FROM PRACTICE

My old teaching coach had advised me sharply to stay in the same room with the kids. It was good advice for half a career. Then, suddenly, it was not enough. Imagine me, a high school teacher in mid-career. Something in the air has set me off: public images of the teacher as dunce, of curriculum as pablum, of school as a vacuous ritual. Some things closer and indistinct disturb me, too—the chronic messiness of daily practice, a slow evaporation of career ideals. After fifteen years or so of this work, am I really any good at it? What have I learned from teaching? Apart from the peripheral things, the cynical things, the technical things, what do I know? These questions seize me at breakfast, and in the middle of a morning's teaching, and even sometimes in dreams. I sense that I must answer them or quit teaching.

Stepping Outside

I had begun my career flushed with my generation's swollen sense of virtue and accomplishment. Immaturity had its function. The sense of virtue oriented me from the start to the moral dimensions of teaching, made me skeptical from the start of merely technical conceptions of teaching. The swollen sense of accomplishment supplied enough ego to bridge years of craftlessness. Numbing the pain of one or two unruly classes a day and of chronic uncertainty about what to teach tomorrow, ego salvaged my zeal to make a difference in the world through teaching. Most of the kids liked me, and I liked them. If I was learning the ropes now, it was only so I could rehang them later.

Then, after a few years, I acquired some craft. Like a cultivated enclosure in the wilderness, however, this craft magnifed the aura of what surrounded it. So my increasing success called special attention to my failures. They were still frequent. Why was I seldom certain about what to teach or when to teach it, about what was ever really learned, about how to manage the conflicts before me—often even the simplest of them?

Reasonably enough, though also blindsidedly, I blamed the conditions of my work, and I looked for a better place to work. Happily, in those days of teacher shortage, I found one: a small public high school where collegiality was the norm—an uncommon characteristic of schools then and now. There, over the course of the next eight years, my colleagues and I asked one another questions about teaching, talked about teaching techniques, collaborated in teaching, observed one another's teaching, and even evaluated it. At a crucial juncture in my career, I had access to practice other than my own. The consequence is that my craft grew more abundantly than it otherwise might have. I realize now, however, that it grew without my thinking very much about what *it* was. In particular, I never took much notice of the persistence of failure amid growth and of what this might signify.

Then, suddenly, in the early 1980s, the alarms sounded. Schools are putting the nation's security at risk, trumpeted one. High schools have become shopping malls, declared another. A national newsweekly put a duncecapped teacher on its cover. On one level, I took the criticism as a trick to displace economic and social anxiety onto the schools. On another level, I was unnerved. The criticism seemed, somehow, especially aimed at me. By then, I thought, I ought to have become a better teacher—by which I meant, a more certain teacher.

In this state, I happened upon an essay by Israel Scheffler (1984). Responding to the same alarms, he urged policy makers to treat teachers for once as subjects rather than objects—as thinkers, actors, and imaginers, rather than the butt or the tools of change. This he called "hearing teachers in their own voice." I received the phrase like a mysterious gift. Somehow, it suggested to me that I might know more about teaching than I thought I knew, but in a way that was different from what I expected.

By various means, over the next several years, I tried to discover my own teacher's voice—to hear it softly in my work, then transform it into something I could read; which is to say, something I could puzzle over, learn from, show to others. This meant, for one thing, that I had to come to terms with the limits of the advice my old teaching coach had supplied. It was time for me to step outside the room, to learn to hold my worklife at a distance. Some distance, however slight, is crucial for reading: Apartness turns life to text. So I started to keep a professional journal—the first one I had kept since I was a student teacher. Each entry, jotted down as I rode a trackless trolley home from work each day, provided a quick snapshot of the day's teaching—what I said to Kristin, how James looked, the attitude that overcame me as I heard the excuses about the homework, the conflicts I felt about the poem I'd taught. This jotting down was my apartness strategy: to turn into text what was otherwise ephemeral and elusive. Meanwhile, I also undertook some reading *about* teaching—virtually the only noncurricular reading about teaching I'd done since I was a beginning teacher. Then I had been eager for the latest story of how some other beginner had saved a roomful of kids from an oppressive system. Now I was eager for any writing that acknowledged the intricacies of the work and the scarcity of miracles. Happily, I found some writing like this—not much at first, but enough.

This is the gist of reading teaching, its minimal core: to step outside the room, figuratively speaking, and to search for perspective on the events inside. It is simple work on its face, private and comparatively safe, the consequence perhaps of deliberately noticing one's own practice in the eyes of a student teacher, of undertaking some classroom research, even—as in my case—of keeping a simple journal and doing a little theoretical browsing. By such means, teachers may spot the uncertainty in their own practice. They may spot it, as I did, in unexpected tangles of conflicting values, in stubborn ambivalence, in a surprising prevalence of half-steps. Evidence of these and other uncertain things fills the texts of Chapter 3.

Though simple work on its face, as I say, this reading work is also powerful. Schön (1983, 1987) calls it the work of the reflective practitioner and offers convincing evidence of its power. I would say that it is powerful insofar as it sketches the outlines of a craft identity: the gathering sense that teaching does more than apply knowledge, that it transforms knowledge inside the wild triangle of its relations. This is what I gained from my trolley journal. But the work is as painful as it is powerful, especially when undertaken, as in my case, just when one thinks certainty must finally be near.

Reading Together

The pain that accompanies first efforts to read teaching may cause the reader to seek some company to ease it. Among company, one can also figure out the hardest things more easily. So, several months into the keeping of my trolley journal, I found myself among reading company. We called ourselves the Secondary Study Group, and we gathered regularly to talk about teaching, to share our reactions to reading about teaching, and to tell one another stories from teaching. Chapter 4 tells the story of this group, which is a story of self-discovery and of political awakening. It is also an account of a still deeper engagement with reading teaching. What happens on this deeper level is that the uncertainties that elude the grasp of private introspection—on a trolley or anywhere else—become group problems. The conversation they provoke amplifies individual interpretation and builds a sense of professional community. Why does Catherine think she is not working when she is working at her best? What is the work of teaching anyway—this work *we* do? Why does Elizabeth's student accuse her of not looking like a teacher? How does a teacher look? How do *we* as teachers look? Why is Ruth so affected by the accusation she reports? What is the source of *our* vulnerability?

Reading teaching together is much harder than reading it alone, however. It requires finding and inventing ways to put aside the pretensions and fears that keep most teachers behind closed doors, or else chatting about everything but work while in one another's company. It entails confronting the silence of teaching. This is the silence that rises from the cells—the semi-autonomous, semi-detachable teaching "stations" that define the structure of most schools (Lortie, 1975). The cellular design of schools is a structural response to historically unbridled growth in the student population and historically high turnover rates among teachers. The cellular design permits a school to grow or diminish by this teacher or that without much organizational consequence. Of course, the design itself has great organizational consequence, including the empowerment of those who coordinate the cells, the subordination of those who inhabit them, and, as Lortie particularly notes, the disparagement of cooperation, inquiry, collegiality, and participation in the fashioning of a schoolwide culture—silence, in short. In the cellular school, teachers are severely isolated from one another during the bulk of their working days. As Sarason (1971), Jackson (1968), Little (1982), and others have suggested, teachers may even fail to develop a language in which to talk about their essentially private work.

To understand the relationship between overcoming this silence and learning to read teaching, it helps to take a feminist view. The authors of *Women's Ways of Knowing* (Belenky, Clinchy, Goldberger, & Tarule, 1986) say that the women whose lives they researched "repeatedly used the metaphor of voice to depict their intellectual and ethical development," that for these women, "the development of a sense of voice, mind, and self were intricately intertwined" (p. 18). One of the women, whom the researchers classify as having recently found a voice, also reveals how vision may be a consequence of voice. She speaks in strongly visual images of tensions that have arisen in her marriage as a result of her new capacity to speak up:

> "We now view events that happen in our lives very differently. He reads them very straightforward, on a superficial kind of level. And I don't. I probe them. I read into them. He says he sees things in black and white and I see all kinds of shades of grays—all these gradations he doesn't see." (p. 147)

"I read into them," she says, and defines a certain level of reading. On this level, the reader combines voice and vision, probes with the confidence that comes from being part of a community. On this level, one has heart enough to see "in all kinds of shades of gray."

Going Back Inside the Triangle

On the other hand, reading teaching among company—even perceptively and critically—is not enough. What is the point, after all, of raising one's consciousness? What does the woman who has found a voice do with it? Does she keep her marriage as it is? And, if not, what kind of marriage does she want?

At some point, the teacher who has dared to read teaching must also, I think, dare to make that reading serve the interests of kids. Having gained some perspective by reading alone, and having gained some power by reading together, the reader must find a way to take the perspective and the power back inside the triangle—the wildly uncertain triangle defined by the teacher's own ambivalent self, that bunch of unpredictable kids, and the always slippery subject. On the personal level, this means not only having some understanding of the work one does but also using that understanding to transform the work and its effectiveness. On the professional level, it means having not only reflective teachers for our schools but also thoughtful schools for them to work in.

So back inside the triangle, reading teaching involves an effort to recognize both the complex systems that enmesh the school and the opportunities the teacher has to use and confront them in the interests of kids. It means not only tolerating the uncertainty of teaching but also using that uncertainty to unsettle kids' views in the face of big, uncertain questions. This demands all the energy one can muster to stay materially in touch with the moods and moves of kids, to remember the perspectives one has gathered on the outside, to avoid the silence of the cells. It demands courage to question authority and traditions and to try new ways of working. Finally, it demands an ear for the voice that Scheffler meant, a call down the years to hold together the wild triangle that wants so much to split apart.

Duckworth (1991), in an essay that celebrates complexity in knowing, offers us a glimpse of the demands that even a single moment of reading teaching on the inside may make on a teacher, and from this glimpse we may infer the rewards. In this case the teacher is Lisa Schneier, whose uncertain triangle on this particular day features *Romeo and Juliet* and a bunch of ninth graders struggling to read it aloud and bring it to life. In the middle of the struggle, one boy, playing Romeo in the balcony scene, suddenly breaks off his reading and confronts Schneier: "He loves her. *That's* what he's saying. So why all that other stuff? . . . Why can't he just say what he means?" (Schneier, 1990). Duckworth, as if stepping in for Schneier, responds: "That's what he *is* doing: 'what he means' is complex" (p. 8). An excellent answer, though as Duckworth would appreciate, a lot easier to deliver a year later in an essay than in the heat of the moment—with the class watching and the fate of a lesson plan hanging in the balance. Nonetheless, reading teaching on the inside means sensing the opportunity of such moments, even though they are thrust at one suddenly. The teacher as reader senses that this may be her best chance in a year to teach all the kids in this room right now what "meaning" is and how it relates to—among other things—poetry. Although she also senses in the same instant that it may just as easily invite a fruitless digression, a bad break in the group's momentum, she decides to go for it anyway—the possible gain is worth the risk. Besides, she knows how to recover momentum. Reading teaching at this level of engagement is what Myles Horton (1990) would call "two-eyed reading"— one eye on the kids as they really are in all their manifold selves, one eye on what they might become with the right help, push, and faith. In this case, they might become kids who really know what *meaning* means: What a boon for all of us to have such kids in our communities.

THEORETICAL PERSPECTIVES

First, a paradoxical thought: To gain a sense of teaching's complexity, one has to simplify its terms. Teaching is vast. It ranges from a mother's relationship with her infant to the supervision of someone's doctoral dissertation, from some instance in which the teacher harangues a cowering group to another in which the teacher fails through excessive tenderness to have any effect at all. To cope with its vastness, one has to compare teaching to something simpler: It is like conveying, like selling, like gardening, like coaching, like conducting a religious revival, like hosting a TV talk show. Depending upon the operative simile, one may fall under the sway here of a particular discipline, each a great system of simplification. Economics, with its eye for efficiency; philosophy, with its moral and epistemological interests; psychology, with its focus on cognition or the behavior of individuals and groups; and anthropology, with its concern for culture—all play important roles in how many of us think about teaching today, both when we think about it rigorously in some research program and even when we think about it casually.

Without in any way disputing the value of any other discipline in thinking about teaching, this book proposes a place for the discipline of textual criticism—a technical name for close reading.[1] Textual criticism is as reductive, as much a simplifying system as any other discipline, of course. Like the others it excludes much more of the lived life of teaching practice than it includes (Buchmann, 1984). The reason why I urge it upon us nonetheless is that I think we desperately need what it happens especially to include. Textual criticism is founded upon a method that is sensitive to voice, as well as to conflict and ambiguity, layered meaning, and the pervasive presence of ideology. A *text* in textual criticism is a meaningful construction whose meaning arises from the interplay of several forces: an author's intentions, a reader's response, the echoes of other texts alluded to deliberately or not, the frictions and connections and collisions that occur among all the signs within the text, and the ideologies inescapably present below the surface of these signs. A text can be a literary one in the conventional sense—a poem or a novel; or it may be another kind of text—a film, an ad, a folk song, a private diary, a political manifesto. From the perspective of this book, texts may include a teacher's journal, transcribed conversations among teachers, stories and arguments about school policy, and books written by teachers.

Why study teaching so indirectly when one can just as well observe it directly? The answer I propose is that what may be indirect may also be, if closely read, richly revealing. In fact, all access to teaching is mediated. The observers' eyes are not a neutral channel, as every watched teacher suspects. And certainly the statistician's figures are not neutral, emphasizing, as they do, the evident over the contingent: James as a score on an achievement test, rather than the bundle of impulsive behavior before me. An access to teaching that is mediated by teachers themselves offers opportunities not only to see what is shown but to study how and why it is shown, and thereby to glimpse what teachers value, what they choose to frame and fail to frame, what they know, and what deep forces influence them. Sometimes a single image yields rich meaning, both interpreted within its own context and read critically against other texts and contexts. The recurrence of images, motives, and themes across multiple texts offers the study of teaching a resource of great value, though its validity remains local rather than universal. This is because the textual critic, unlike the social scientist searching for generalizations across cases, pays as much attention to the differences within recurrence as to the similarities, and delights in anomaly: those moments that stand out unaccountably. One consequence is that insight achieved by means of the close reading of texts may seem uncompelling by other disciplinary lights and disparaged as merely anecdotal. By literary light, however, the anecdote is fundamental. If it fails the test of science, then that is part of its claim on our attention: It provides another window. As Foucault (1980) explains, this window is superbly situated for glimpsing important knowledge that has been disqualified as being below acceptable standards for truth, that has been declared naive. Thoughtful teachers have long suspected that their deepest knowledge has been declared naive.

Even when we choose to observe teaching directly, we may do well to think of what we are observing as itself a kind of text.[2] The teacher authors a community of struggle and growth that we call a course in algebra or the third grade but shares the work of constructing its meaning with its principal readers, the students. With their connivance and often against their resistance, the teacher builds a text from the elements of the classroom medium: time, space, talk, task. She draws in the process upon the codes of teaching. These include method codes: arrangements of timing and stance; habits of presentation and evaluation; mechanisms of control and release. They also include subject codes: what literature is and is not, what history does and does not cover, how math is done, how settled a science is, and so forth. The teacher improvises in the face of the powerful and intrusive context that rings and often permeates the work. Her students do as well. In the end, she cannot control this text amid the swirling and immensely uncertain influences, yet she takes responsibility, signs her name to it. This is a useful way to think about teaching insofar as it acknowledges that the construction of the "meaning" of classroom experience is beyond the teacher's control, but also insofar as it holds the teacher's voice and the teacher's passion as central.[3]

Three Elements of Reading Teaching

If teaching is a text, then it is a fast and evanescent one, authored serially minute by minute. It may be said to linger overnight in the memories and homework of both teacher and students, or in the air of the classroom—as any teacher knows who has stayed past closing time on a Friday, or returned for some forgotten sheaf of papers on a Sunday. Still, it is only air, and holds only so long—as any teacher knows, too, who has returned to the classroom in, say, mid-July, when the papers on the wall or in the desks seem forlorn and the creaks in the floor alien among the sounds of summer outside. Reading such a text, then, must be a matter of turning air into something more tangible. Hence the observer's notes.

Teachers themselves can engage in this *textmaking*. Textmaking is what I, who am the trolley-riding reader of my own teaching in the next chapter, did on the trolley. It is what my colleagues and I deliberately sought to do in the Secondary Study Group, when, as you will see in Chapter 4, we first decided to tape-record our stories and conversations about teaching. This is what we did at Bright High School when the teachers there and I began to chronicle the school policy story that is retold and reread in Chapter 5. And this is what Margaret Haley, Sylvia Ashton-Warner, and Eliot Wigginton did when they, the teacher-writers of Chapter 6, sat down to write their autobiographical books. This is what thousands of teacher-writers do when they keep teaching journals or simply take notes on their teaching in the interest of providing material for some later autobiography or contribution to a teacher periodical. This is what a few, such as Vivian Paley (1979, 1981, 1988), do when they turn on tape recorders in their classrooms. This is what some, such as Chris Zajac, do when they admit writers into their classrooms (Kidder, 1989). This is what many do who videotape their teaching or allow others to do so (Goldman, 1990; Sato, 1989).

Besides textmaking, reading teaching on all levels also involves what I call *gripping*. The metaphor is meant to suggest that teaching, even when rendered tangible in the form of a text—whether diary entry, bit of videotape, or other artifact of the actual process—still wants to be running off. What the reader of teaching must do is to hold it steady, often by bringing it into the grip of some set of ideas, some perspective, some value—often supplied by some other text (Scholes, 1985). The point of this gripping is not to capture the teaching in some pure state—to give it a "timeless" reading, so to speak. That is as silly and futile a gesture when the text is teaching as when it is *Antigone*. The point is rather, by means of some external point of reference, to inquire about the text's status in time: At this moment, in this cultural milieu, amid these circumstances, as compared or contrasted to this point of reference, what does this text mean? Chapter 4, for example, recounts how, one evening, the Secondary Study Group managed a close and productive reading of a difficult and slippery text drawn from one member's experience, by holding it in the grip of some other texts and of some ideological fragments.

Finally, besides textmaking and gripping, reading teaching demands *doubting*. This is the emotional antonym of the believing that teachers rely upon to sustain their teaching (Elbow, 1986). In even the most courageous and reflective teaching, believing takes precedence over doubting in the sense that the teacher tempers his or her believing with doubt, not the other way around. Of course, the reflective teacher faces up to failure every time he or she reads a set of student papers, or thinks rigorously about what Carmen and Eric have actually learned, or dares to subject bright plans to critical light. But then, at least in the best circumstances, he or she returns wholeheartedly to believing in the papers' signs of progress, in Carmen's and Eric's potential to pull through, and in the efficacy of the plans. In the end, belief predominates. This is why traces of believing course through every text drawn from teaching. They are traces of the teacher's investment of self—a self full of conflicted values and dispositions, one that is gendered and historically conditioned and laden with ideologies professed and unprofessed.

Reversing the emphasis of teaching itself, doubt takes precedence in reading teaching. The reader of any text must let doubt have an edge over belief in order to gain the upper hand in the experience; otherwise the reader cannot be said to be reading at all, but rather undergoing manipulation by a text. What is wanted is what has been called "critical thinking"—a capacity to make up one's mind apart from any text's persuasion. When the text to be read is drawn from one's own teaching, however, this process is difficult and painful—as Chapter 3 reveals—because doubting what one must also believe involves a kind of contortion. Even when the text is drawn from another's work, reading teaching takes some courage: an almost physical capacity to ride the thrust of the other's story, yet hold oneself apart from it. This is why some teachers experience discomfort reading others' accounts of teaching or even observing others teach.

Three Disclaimers

Reading teaching is not a panacea. It can help in the struggle to achieve reflective practice, professional renewal, and school reform—but only in contexts also rich in vision, leadership, pluck, and luck. Reading teaching is not a fancy method, requiring special expertise or training. It depends upon simple if neglected things like noticing, writing, talking, listening, and, of course, reading itself. Finally, reading teaching is not a novel method. It has been around as long as teaching has, though somehow our profession has recently permitted other methods to acquire more status. It seems to me time to correct the resulting imbalance.

3

Reading on the Trolley

In 1984, in my fifteenth year of teaching, I raised my own teacher's voice and turned it into text for reading. I wanted to know what reading might reveal that doing had not. So, while riding the trackless trolley each day from school to a graduate course I was taking, I sometimes jotted down a description of a teaching experience I had had that day—usually only one, often one that surprised or puzzled me. These jottings were irregular, only twenty-one in all between December and May, mostly written in the squiggly hand of a trolley rider. In this chapter, I present excerpts from these old readings, thickened by another textual layer, a current rereading: text upon a text.

I begin the close readings of this book with this most personal one to back up my view that teaching is personal, that the person of the teacher is its root. This sounds trite, until one considers how little writing about teaching, and research and policy making about teaching, considers the role in it of the individual teacher's gender and class, of the teacher's moral vision and intentions, of the teacher's own felt conflicts and tenderness, of the contrivances of the teacher's person that become the teacher's persona. Rather than seeing teaching as rooted in the person of the teacher, we are much more apt to see it as rooted in some philosophical, political, or bureaucratic imperative, with the person of the teacher just the last bit of branch supporting the leaf. The result is a loss of liveliness in our sense of the teacher's relation to students and subject. A view of teaching that takes the teacher's self seriously—in all its commitment, ambivalence, and contrivance—necessarily also takes seriously the sources of this self's construction in the lively uncertainties associated with the teacher's students and subject. As a close reading reveals, my journal is about a *me* that I create day by day to connect *them* and *it*—a *me* that is, because of this connecting work it does, more irresolute than other *me*'s. Teaching is not like building bridges between stable points, but like building flexible webs among constantly moving points—among, for example, the evanescent images of a poem and twenty-two different minds, including mine.

I read my own teaching first for another reason, too. Teaching, closely read, is messy: full of conflict, fragmentation, and ambivalence. These conditions of uncertainty present a problem in a culture that tends to regard conflict as distasteful and that prizes unity, predictability, rational decisiveness, certainty. This is a setup: Teaching involves a lot of "bad" stuff, yet teachers are expected to be "good." Of all the problems that plague the work of teaching, it seems to me the worst is that teachers are subject to a spuriously binary valuation system. Everybody thinks teachers are either good or bad: principal, parents, the school reform consultant, the local teacher educator, the kids, the teacher's colleagues, even the teacher. In her research of another binary system that plagues us, Dweck (1987) found that children who believe that a person is either smart or dumb will tend to avoid challenges that may reveal which of the two they themselves are. The irony is that it is precisely by means of such challenges that one builds intelligence. Something like the same thing may happen in teaching. Teachers may avoid reflection and collegiality in order to avoid revealing to themselves and others whether they are good or bad teachers. The irony is that it is only by means of reflection and collegiality that one can learn to see beyond "good" and "bad."

By reading my own teaching first, I mean to take the heat first. I lay it out right from the start: I am not a good teacher, I am not a bad teacher. In the textualized bits of it that follow, as in all my teaching, I am a teacher grappling with an enormously complex task; savoring what I take to be wins, enduring what are undoubtedly losses; managing well sometimes, managing poorly often; beset by ambivalence, prejudice, ego, and a number of other "faults" that my reading may not have uncovered but that yours will—all of them associated with uncertainty.[1]

December 11

Holly and James dominated my teaching today in Writing. I wanted to push James as tenderly and helpfully as I could, partly because I wanted him to succeed and partly because I wanted Holly to know that I pushed kids. She seems so far to be an aggressive learner, and I did not want her to think that the milieu of my class discouraged aggressive learning or tolerated the numb, blocked passivity now besetting James. I almost said to James that I wanted to put a firecracker up his ass, and I almost said that there was nothing I could do if he refused to get engaged. But I only said half of the former (putting a firecracker on his chair), and I did not say the latter at all, feeling that it might seem to say that I had given up on him.

Holly was new to the class. She was bright and beautiful. I imagined that she had had to stave off some negative reaction among her peers and mine in order to move into this class, which was nontracked and heterogeneous, quite different from the upper-track classes she was used to. When she arrived, she became at once for me, though the thought may never even have crossed her mind, a monitor of the rigor of my teaching aims and methods, an incarnation of the newly critical public. I report no feelings of "tender" helpfulness toward her, just apparent wariness. Nor do I "push" her, just let her know "that I push kids." So I do not touch her in the metaphorical sense, whereas I do the other kids, and speak here metaphorically of raping James, though when I spoke in class I suggested that the firecracker could do its work without my touching.

I cannot any longer remember James. Quite unlike Holly's, his face and his identity have receded from my mind. What remains is this record that I simultaneously felt tenderness and hostility toward him on one December morning. The hostility is perhaps due to the fact that, unlike Holly, he seems to me more a part of the problem than of the solution. The problem, of course, is whatever has set off the alarm: high school in crisis, teaching bankrupt. The duncecapped teacher haunts me. The tenderness I report is due perhaps to the fact that I identify with James as a victim and so sympathize with his resistance, though I also mean to quash it. The passage hints at how I hold these feelings in tension, perhaps productive tension from James's point of view.

Why do I say that "I push kids"—why this physical, even violent metaphor, pushed itself to the extreme in the firecracker image? I think the answer is complex. I myself felt pushed and frustrated by James's passive resistance. He is "numbed" and "blocked," but these problems are not his alone. They are mine, too, by virtue of our relationship. The newly critical public wants teachers to feel accountable, so I will be accountable—I will explode the blockage, find a way into James, try to connect his creativity with the world I mean to enact for him in my classroom. But this image, violent and sexual as it is, must also be read as blocked itself—both by a countervailing feeling of tenderness and by a censoring tongue.

Still, it is a very male image. Reading it years later helps me wonder, with feminist interest, about all my teaching. Images of teaching that I find more appealing than this one explicitly acknowledge the role of conflict in learning without inevitably situating it between learner and teacher. I think of metaphors for teaching I have heard some women use: McIntosh's (1990) teaching as gardening, whereby the teacher prepares the ground for growth and strives to respect each student's way of blooming, but in a garden full of struggle; or Wehmiller's (1985) miracle of the bread dough rising, whereby the teacher's work involves long and patient kneading, followed by stillness, but a stillness in which the dough rises by virtue of tiny chemical explosions prepared by kneading. In each case, conflict is mediated, deliberately contrived to happen at a distance from a core relationship of caring.

December 12

The Shari episode seems to have worked out OK. Today she was able to share her work with the class without demanding an inappropriate amount of the class's attention. At least we managed to avoid the kind of struggle for attention that made last Friday's class so difficult. I think my gut instinct was right on Friday to maintain a little distance between me and Shari's hurt feelings.

Kristin made fun of me today for using my hands too much. I stopped using them then, and she told me that the energy made my shoulders shake and my body rock; she said I might as well go back to using my hands.

Shari was blind, and my teaching had a strong visual dimension. This mismatch was a source of problems. In fact it was Kristin who helped me discover this. "Shari doesn't know when you're only kidding," she told me after class one day, "because only your eyes say you're kidding." I was often stern in my voice, but playful in my eyes, a crucial tension in my teaching that Shari could not notice. For her the sternness had no softener. Nor could she see the clownish enthusiasm in my hands, or in my shoulders when I kept my hands still—enthusiasm which was doubtlessly in tension, too, with a softly serious voice.

Kristin's experiment in which she concluded that my hands were an outlet for some deeper energy was one of a number of incidents that occurred about this time—others involving Kristin, too—that revealed to me a difference between *me* teaching, and *me* at other times—a persona constructed of, among other things, fast hands, playful eyes, and a softly serious voice.

December 13

I trusted a very loose process today, and saw kids showing some self-direction. Every one of my Writing kids had a project underway. I also kept in check my ordinary tendency to offer more advice than they either ask for or can probably handle at the moment. I realized for once that I ought to let them set the agenda for my conferences with them. I have to admit, however, that in the process I had to suppress a few of my own yawns.

There are six *I*'s in these five brief sentences. In this respect, the text reflects its referent, the morning's teaching, which was pervaded by ego, albeit ego under wraps. I felt that if I showed an exuberant self this particular morning, I might rob my kids of their own selves. I had to suppress my self, letting some excess energy erupt in a few stifled yawns. Even undercover, however, ego was still my main tool. I saw *them* in terms of *me:* Now they needed less of me; tomorrow, maybe a bit more.

To say one uses one's self in teaching, however, is not the same thing as to say that one *is* oneself in teaching. The exuberance I may choose either to express or to suppress when I teach is not quite authentically *my* exuberance. Although I feel it genuinely, it is nonetheless an artifact of a role I play.[2] I first realized this when I visited a third-grade classroom where my wife was the teacher. There I saw cute little kids, about whom I already knew a lot from dinnertime conversations. But the woman teaching them, whose dinnertime talk about them had conditioned my perception of them, clearly was not treating them in school as cute little kids. There they were responsible people. To this extent, I remember thinking, she was not quite my wife now but rather their teacher. My colleague Margaret Metzger once remarked that she always has a few students whom she would detest if they were not her students, but whom she regards warmly and tolerantly because they are her students.

But what is the self one uses in teaching? What is its function? How is it constructed? There are only the briefest clues in the passage above, though there are others later on in the trolley journal. Here one reads that the self is functional even when it is purposely undisplayed, suggesting that its function is catalytic, mediational. It seems constructed in this case of intertextual elements: I handle my*self* as I do here, probably because of what I have read or heard somewhere about teaching writing.

December 21

On the last day before Christmas break, I teach Capote's "A
Christmas Memory." I simply read the whole nine pages of it
aloud—after an enthusiastic promotion of it, telling them how
much it means to me, how beautiful it is, and how (seeking to
arouse their curiosity) its author recently died, an alcoholic
wreck. Throughout my reading of it, I worry that I'll break into
tears—when the dog dies; when Buddy must leave home; when
his friend grows too old to exclaim, "It's fruitcake weather";
when she goes on a few years more baking cakes with Queenie
only, then alone; when she tells Buddy that flying kites together
is like seeing God. In fact, I did grow tearful near the end of the
reading—as I'm tearful now as I write this. I'm sure the kids could
hear my tearfulness in my voice.

Now the point of this entry is that my method was not
"good"—reading to kids for 45 minutes is not a recommended
method—I'd never do it, for example, if I were being observed.
And not only is the method not good, but, in a fundamental
sense, neither is my objective. That is, I surely wanted today to
use this piece to transfer my feelings directly from me to the kids.
But that didn't work, as I knew—both theoretically and practical-
ly, too—it could not. But I am convinced that what transferred
was not the content of my feelings but rather the experience of
contact with commitment. The kids experienced how much I
loved this piece; they got to participate in my interest, observe its
effects. And ultimately I think this teaches them something quite
important—more important than any one short story. What
counts is not the literature itself, but our commitment to it, our
engagement with it, its effects on us and our experience.

I use rational, technical language here—my *method* is not good,
neither is my *objective*. What I mean, though, is that I think the
relations of this lesson may have failed. I had wanted to attract my
students to Capote's skillful writing by means of my own strong attrac-
tion to it. The students had themselves just written autobiographical
essays like Capote's. We called them Velcro essays: sticking little memory narratives together to make big ones. Capote does it superbly.

"Come tour this model with me," I tell my students in effect. "Let
me show you, merely by means of the appreciation you'll hear in my
reading voice, how the author uses bits of theme to link incidents in a
chain of childhood memories." One may call this a selection of teach-

ing objectives and methods, but the phrase seems too cold, too instrumental. I myself am a method here.

Perhaps my reading of this lesson's effect on my students was
correct. Or perhaps they just quietly tolerated what they took to be
my strange intimacy with an essay they felt indifferent about. In any
case, the taste of this lesson lingers with me still. It is the taste of a
failed relation. I was swept up by the power of my teaching past the
bounds of my ordinary judgment, defended the teaching to myself
despite my own clear sense of its faults, felt compelled to write out
that long sequence of moments that nearly made me weep, and in the
process nearly wept again.

Now, remote from tears, I think as I reread this text how powerful
a teacher's belief in his teaching can be. I could not come down from
mine even on the trolley, though doubts began to creep in then as a
result of my textualizing. And, in the end, doubts about this lesson are
what I remember most. The result is that my memory of the incident
has become an exemplar, a constituent element of my practical judgment as a teacher. It does not, of course, provide a rule. I will probably
teach this way again, and it may even work next time; but I certainly
will not choose to do so without thinking first of this time when it did
not work.

In an aside within the passage, I say that I would never teach this
way under observation. Alone, I let myself do what some normative
sense, conditioned by ideology as well as practical judgment, suggests
I should not do. I experiment, protected by my isolation, and my
remark affords a glimpse of isolation's strong hold on teaching.

December 31

I am sitting here marking long essays. All the kids so far seem
to have worked hard. But I definitely see my standard of what's
high quality—an *A* paper—shifting to accommodate what I know
to be the kid's strengths. I'm looking to see *stretching*—stretching
of existing limits. When I see good evidence of stretching, then I
award an *A*. Now the question on my mind is whether a neutral
observer would see comparable worth in all the papers I mark *A*?

These are the Velcro papers that Capote modeled for. I am reading
them on New Year's Eve. More than a week has passed since I last saw
my kids, last weaved any of the web I had been weaving before the
holiday break: the one connecting me, them, Capote, and other elements of the subject we were studying. Maybe the time gap has em-

boldened me to ask the question that seems suddenly to seize my grading pencil. How has the web affected my judgment? What would a neutral observer think who had not spent time with the authors of these Velcro papers?

I say that I look for "stretching." I have seen these papers at an earlier stage of development and have heard parts of them read aloud in class; thus I have a sense of the distance between where they have been and where they are now. I have a sense also of where they ought to be pointed—toward Capote, presumably. I sit at my kitchen table, lending, say, half an hour to each paper, and I try to construe what is beyond my power to construe with even minimal certainty: the progress of each kid's writing development, the worthiness of each paper in terms of broad standards for autobiographical writing, the resolution of the conflict I feel between my responsibility to believe in each kid and my commitment to hold each to a high standard. And I think I succeed. I invent a gestalt for each of my encounters with a Velcro paper on this last afternoon of the year, and I label the gestalt with a letter grade. The trouble, however, is that the gestalts do not sort reliably—one named *A* seems unlike another named *A*.

A benefit of ferreting out some instances of uncertainty in teaching is that they may help us discern the deficits of the structures in which we typically teach. Actually, the full entry for December 31 does not stop with the question, as this excerpt does. It goes on to a smug answer. I placate the monster I've briefly stirred with another donation of certainty. Yet it is probably not just my kids who are stretching, but my standards, too. Perhaps they are stretching quite out of shape. I cannot, in fact, put myself at the center of a web and stand outside it, too. Why should I have to? Why can't I share the burdens of creating and maintaining standards with colleagues? What are departments for? This is another glimpse of isolation's hold on teaching, but from a different perspective.

January 2

First day back to teaching after holiday break. Kristin told me I ought to take lecithin to help me with my short-term memory. I certainly do have some trouble keeping track of what seems like the mountain of details that I have to attend to each period. To-day: two sets of papers to hand out, three sets of copies of student papers to read, homework to remember to take time to assign, make-up tests to hand out to kids who didn't take the test before vacation, books that we've finished that still haven't been collected, reminders to particular kids about assignments they're miss-

ing, a note to myself to remember to do something tonight, col-
lecting back papers to put in kids' files. At the end of every class,
there are always piles of things on my teaching table that have to
be sorted, filed, carted back to my desk, etc. Sometimes I just sigh
wearily when I look at all of it, and many times I simply walk
away from it for awhile to catch my breath and gather some energy for dealing with it.

But my interest here is not to write about managing details as
a particular part of the craft of teaching. Of course, this is absolutely true, obviously true. But I want to say that I think mis-
managing them just a little is part of *my* teaching craft. I mean
that I've created a classroom persona and one characteristic of
that persona is that it needs lecithin. I might force myself to manage more efficiently the endless details of my teaching—but if efficiency rather than mild inefficiency were part of my persona,
I might become coldly efficient. Efficiency might take over,
might control my teaching. Or I might take more care to avoid details.

But part of my teaching style, one of the important ways I
seek to keep my teaching energetic and exciting for kids, is to
keep a dozen little pots simmering at once. That means details,
and the number of details requires this persona or some other.

I'm reminded of Lampert's idea of a teaching persona as a
means for reconciling irreconcilable things, for holding together
the experience of teaching and learning in a classroom. *Persona*
is a good word for this thing because this thing masks the reality
that is inevitably a confused tangle of learning objectives and
learning achievements. *Persona* suggests that there is some unify-
ing emotion/experience/sense/order. Both teacher and students
trust the persona, though all know it is a mask.

Lampert is Magdalene Lampert, a teacher-researcher, and at this
point I had just read her essay entitled "How Do Teachers Manage to
Teach? Perspectives on Problems in Practice" (1985). I was still bask-
ing in what I took to be its revelation: that teaching is inherently messy
at its heart, that it is a kind of perpetual tidying up of the surface of
chaos, that the messiness I have always felt in my work is not my fault
but rather the work's essential condition. I had read a great deal about
teaching before I read Lampert, but I had never read anything like this,
or had at least never been ripe to comprehend anything like this.

That is how reading teaching sometimes works: Texts intersect to
create self-revelation. Here the texts are my written record of a brief

instance of my own teaching, including Kristin's half-serious joke and Lampert's essay. In the background, too, are others not mentioned: especially a book by Berlak and Berlak (1981) about dilemmas in teaching, one that Lampert's footnotes drew me to; and also a remembered remark, the stunning remark of a friend who, upon reading Lampert, exclaimed, "How dare she call this 'Managing to Teach'—it's not about *managing* at all—it's about failing to manage!"

My little epiphany here deals with the teacher's persona, or teaching self as I called it above. I claim that it is a kind of tent meant to shelter irreconcilable elements in teaching—a shelter for uncertainty. Here the irreconcilable elements that take shelter together are insistence and forgiveness. These may be manifestations of a deeper pair, control and caring (Noddings, 1984). I make demands on my students, insist on their diligence; but by a complex means involving this constructed self I display to them, I forgive them in advance for their slippages. My forgetfulness leaves room for them to forget, too, but without suggesting that I expect anything less of them than full remembrance.

January 7

I struggled today with my Writing class. It was a struggle that I know has been building for days. This awful fan in my room is somewhat at fault. The constant white noise is a drain on attention and patience. It makes what otherwise would be harmless, even useful little side conversations destructive of the atmosphere I want to build and hold.

But the question of atmosphere is so obviously a personal one—a product of *my* mood. So, for example, I knew over breakfast this morning that I would have to struggle with my Writing class. Now was that because I knew I was in a struggling mood, or because I knew the last few classes had built this mood in me—so that when I thought of the class, I snapped into the mood?

How I struggle through these situations is interesting. There is much Lampert in it—much fending off of decisive moments, much seeking to hold the coalition.

One wall of my classroom was glass, looking out over the first floor of the school library. Through the glass, my classes and I were always on display to whoever might look up in the middle of rummaging through the *Reader's Guide to Periodical Literature*. The rest of the room was paneled. There was no window that opened to the outside, only a great vent in the ceiling with a large, constantly whirring fan inside. It spilled out hot air on hot spring days and cold air on cold January days like this one.

Setting is important in teaching, of course, and this one on occasion seemed a kind of compression chamber, in which my students and I labored between eyes on one side and noise above. Yet in this entry I nearly blame the vent for a condition that I know has arisen from other sources. I may have been particularly tired that week, just at the moment when my teaching energy may have been most needed. It is a matter of ''mood,'' I say. Seen from the front, January is a long, gray month in school for teachers and for students, who in this case may have egged me on to little bursts of temper, who, I recall now, enjoyed noticing my mood each morning and predicting to themselves how it would color our collective experience. I once jokingly told them that I would buy a gun so that I could blow away the fan—a great image of displaced tension.

January 11

Today I had to ask Rachel to move her seat, then later, Annie, too. Also I had some trouble soliciting volunteers to share their writing. I think some uneasiness has settled into the class, and I'm not sure how to dislodge it. There are distinct groups—for example, the five girls who always sit together, or at least try to (today Shari refused to move her seat so that Kristin could sit as usual among the five). I plunged into the problem at the risk of charges of unfairness. But my instincts were right here, I think now. Some action was called for. Yet the psychological problem of taking action in these situations is that they cannot be neatly, satisfactorily resolved.

Holly has shaken me just a bit. With her there, I think I should be more intellectual, more demanding, less tolerant of common fooling around, and—paradoxically—not petulant and petty, more relaxed, more open. The kids who are cliquish may have turned cliquish because I have turned away from them, distanced myself from them. It's like it was in high school—a new friend with more social status enters my life. Then somehow I find myself with that person in a situation where my older, lower-status friends are, too. Subtly, but unmistakably, I slight the older friends. They resent it. Something like that is going on now.

Context has intruded upon text. One teaches always in a social milieu fraught with many meanings, especially including those related to gender and class. I am a man. All the students I write about above are young women. I teach and they live in a suburb of Boston, a suburb that is often described as working-class in its composition but that is more accurately described as a mixture of people who, regardless of income, either exhibit or do not exhibit middle-class pretensions. Of course, even this division seems simpler than it is, since the ways in which a family or a person may or may not exhibit middle-class pretensions are myriad. Holly's parents, for example, were well-educated intellectuals whose expectations for Holly included graduation from an excellent college. Yet they were poor, partly the consequence of following alternative careers. They liked Holly's interest in my course partly because they liked what they understood my values to be, and partly because they viewed my course as more progressive than other options. I liked their values, too, and I liked the ways they talked and acted. I was, I think, drawn to them and to their daughter as a matter of class.

She was also, as I said above, physically beautiful. The other girls were less conventionally attractive physically; and they all came from homes that were, from the point of view of class, less attractive to me, too, or at least to that part of me with middle-class pretensions. On the other hand, I felt more comfortable with the five. They did not watch my teaching as I imagined that Holly did. The difference here may be class-based as well as sexual. I felt more comfortable with the five because my class background is similar to theirs. They were my sisters when I was in high school, while Holly was the girl I dreamed about but could not be myself with.

January 22

This happened yesterday in Humanities. I had just handed out a test on *Siddhartha*. I had been teaching for a week about Hinduism; we'd had a visitor to lead us in meditation. As she took the test, one girl said quite loudly, "My father thinks you've been giving us some misinformation on Hinduism." The girl next to her asked immediately, excitedly, "Is he? What? What?" whereupon the girl reached into her bag for notes she had taken on what her father had said, while I snapped, "No, I haven't given you misinformation," and then trying to recover, added, "I want to know what your father said, but not now because you have to take the test. We'll talk after you're done."

Then, while the class took the test, I worried about what she'd said. It was true that I was no scholar of Hinduism, that, in fact, my knowledge of it was quite shallow. Should I have avoided teaching something that I was not expert in? I had tried to say "I don't know" whenever students asked questions beyond my competence, but I had also undoubtedly answered a few I shouldn't have answered—questions that demanded that I stretch my thin knowledge too far. Was it an answer to one of these that troubled the girl's father? How serious was my error? And now that the whole class knew that I had erred, did they mistrust all the rest of what I had taught them?

But it's inevitable, I also thought, that a teacher will oversimplify. How can I teach anything if I have to teach it all in its full richness and ambiguity? Don't kids have to have simpler structures to hang ambiguity on before they can deal with it?

It turned out that the girl apologized after the class for saying what she had said. The "misinformation" involved my implication that Hindus took interest in what non-Hindus think or do. Non-Hindus are merely untouchables to Hindus, she told me her father had said. I responded that Hinduism was a very complex phenomenon—that it was surely true that there was much intolerance among Hindus, but that I thought there was great tolerance, too. And I promised to see what I could find out in my sources.

It is not surprising that I found the unnamed girl's remark so threatening, as both she and the girl next to her must immediately have sensed, and as they probably intended. Unexpectedly, at the start of a test—a test being a thing that is supposed to settle uncertainties about what has been taught and what has been learned, that is supposed to quiet kids down and manifest the teacher's power—suddenly, this girl upsets the two key relations of teaching with a single swat. Boom—she doesn't trust me; boom—it's because I don't know what I'm teaching. At the same time, she manages to enhance my vulnerability by imputing the accusation to her father. My classroom door has been opened: Someone outside the intimate circle has evaluated my knowledge of my subject.

Much depends again upon the teacher's believing in his or her own constructions. Just as much depends, however, upon students' capacities to be critical. The consequence is a tension endemic to teaching, one that occasionally flares up as it does here. I have intimidated this girl with my test; she reciprocates rather cleverly. We both manage, however, to regain composure by the end.

January 23

Rick didn't offer his anecdote at last night's Secondary Study Group meeting, but he offered it to me this morning, so I will write it down here and count it as part of last night's proceedings.

He said he had been thinking about what makes the kids listen to him and had decided that when his eyes light up, their eyes light up. He had pondered the difference between those moments when what he says sparks no interest, seems to produce only yawns, and when, on the other hand, it grips kids' attention. The difference comes from getting himself worked up. His voice has to rise in excitement in order to draw in the kids. He said it is like what I told him about my persona of absent-mindedness. He has to act up, put on an act.

I asked about this "putting on an act." Is it only acting, is it phony? No, he said, he has to be genuinely interested in what he's talking about. He gave DNA as an example. He is interested in this subject but has to renew the interest somehow every time he teaches it.

I asked him how he manages to "work" himself up time after time on something like DNA. He said that he thinks about it in his car while driving to school, how remarkable it is, and he works himself up until he's "burning," "on fire," then when he steps into class, his intensity is contagious. He can see the kids' eyes widen as he talks about the subject. The other day, he said, he was so intensely involved in the subject he was teaching, so incredibly worked up, wired, that he fell over a chair near the blackboard on which he was writing furiously, and he actually sailed through the air and onto the floor. I asked him how the kids had reacted. They all laughed, he said. But what was their deeper reaction, I asked. They all knew the intensity I was feeling, he said, and were drawn to it.

The previous night's meeting of the Secondary Study Group, reported in the next chapter, was the first meeting at which we swapped "anecdotes" about teaching. I wondered why Rick had been silent then, so I stopped to talk with him in school the next day. He was not sure, he told me, that his story with its climax of sailing through the air constituted an "anecdote about teaching." He had listened for others that seemed like his but had found none. I think now that this was because the anecdotes offered that night focused on the other key relation of teaching—the one between teacher and students. Rick's is about a fevered relation between teacher and subject that either serves the other relation, as it does here, or else weakens it, makes the teacher seem a fool to his students. The latter possibility provokes my question about his students' reactions to Rick's sail across the room. What did they really think? It was all right, he assures me: They were drawn to his intensity; one relation cultivated the other.

Rick's believing in his teaching is dramatic, captured in his story (or at least my text of it) by metaphors worth noting. Two sets overlap. The first might be called incendiary or electrical: eyes lighting up, sparking interest, gripping attention, wired, burning, on fire, students drawn to a concept like moths to flame. The second set is directional, spatial, but still kinetic: rising in excitement, drawing in kids, acting up, getting worked up, working oneself up, sailing through the air.

As the next two entries show, my conversation with Rick affected my reading of my own teaching even a month later, another lingering intertextual influence—calling special attention, like Lampert's essay, to a certain dimension of my work; infecting me also with its metaphors.

February 25

Today, if only a few more kids had not read *The Metamorphosis,* which I had assigned for vacation reading, I might have succumbed to teacher's despair. Luckily, enough had read it to give me the hope and energy I needed to teach well. Of course, the kids—my partners in this—had more energy too, fresh from vacation—more energy to give to insight, more energy to sustain their patience and their inquiry. I had enough energy to speak slowly and think before speaking, to be flexible with my plans, to respond genuinely to kids' comments, to let the class ride more on the flow of events and talk, to be less controlling and so paradoxically more in control.

February 27

I deliberately decided to make my energy ride high today, like Rick. I simply had a sense that if it flagged even for a moment, that my ability to teach anything worthwhile about *The Tempest* or *The Metamorphosis* would disintegrate. So I pushed myself.

Although I had plans, of course, I didn't particularly follow them. I just used them as a guide in riding the flow of my energy and of the class's responsiveness, of going with the momentum once I'd started a roll. That meant grabbing this or that piece of what I had planned according to the feel of the moment, and using it in an order that intuitively felt right. I remember today, during both classes, deliberately thinking of myself as a kind of impresario, a ring master—not so much genuinely listening to kids' comments, but trying to plug these comments into the larger program at stake and getting them to hear each other.

Echoing Rick, I use the word *energy* seven times across these two short passages. But I have transformed his directional images. Most of his were vertical—getting worked *up*. Two were inwardly horizontal—drawing *in*. Only one—the key one, "sailing through the air"— was at once kinetic, horizontal, and outward. Yet so many of mine are. I am riding, rolling, pushing, following, going with the momentum, fearful of flagging, plugging. The switch from vertical to horizontal imagery signifies a switch from the use of energy solely as propellant to its use as stabilizer, even anti-propellant. As if reversing my jets like an airplane landing, I say, "I had enough energy to speak slowly and to think before speaking."

Then there is the performing metaphor. As ring master or impresario, I use the spotlight to orchestrate the performances of others. Consequently, I do not "genuinely" listen to my students. Rather I assume the ear of the audience, I organize collective hearing but in the process alienate myself from it. To switch to a more contemporary metaphor, I am the TV talk show host whose "listening" is more a visual cue for other listeners than a sign of the real thing.

Once in a conversation with another male teacher, I found myself addressing the question of whether teaching a class was more like having sex or performing theater. Although these three human activities clearly exist on different moral planes, we decided that they also have a lot in common—including caring, skill, intuition, responsiveness, ego, energy, and an ineffable capacity for feeling just right or a bit off. I am reminded of this old conversation when I read what seem to me tacitly sexual metaphors and avowedly theatrical ones in my writing and Rick's talk about teaching. To find an image in more than one text is often to pique interest concerning its presence and variation and is one of the benefits of close reading. So I ask myself what I might otherwise have never asked: Are these just my metaphors? Are they just male metaphors? What are Vivian Paley's favorite metaphors for teaching, or Sylvia Ashton-Warner's? But, whether male or not, what do my metaphors mean?

It is interesting to speculate that they have arisen from another intertextual influence—the crossing of two very different texts in my teaching: Shakespeare's play and Kafka's brief novel. I remember that I taught both these texts as stories of oppression and revolt. Caliban, trapped by the magic of the proto-colonialist Prospero, strikes back by means of connecting gestures that are sexual as well as murderous. Gregor, trapped in an insect body by his own lowly aspirations, strikes back with an attempted kiss—typical catalyst of re-transformation in a fairy tale, but license for family murder here. These are tough texts, and I am teaching them to kids unused to tough texts. I have a feeling, though, that I can turn the rebellious but connecting acts I read in them into classroom connections—students to texts through me. The trick is to energize this *me,* as Rick energized himself teaching about DNA. The sexual and theatrical metaphors signify connecting energy that is present in patience and silence, as well as push and talk.

March 7
        A boy from a nearby town committed suicide yesterday and the fact was reported in today's *Globe.* A girl in my Humanities class asked me to talk a little about it in class. She was clearly moved by it, worried by it, perhaps tempted by it. I promised I would and I did. But the conversation let loose a torrent of strong feelings and debate. The passions were so loud and brash that everybody, including me, was made quite uncomfortable by the class. Kyle talked about how he hated counselors and said dramatically that he'd never tell somebody to see one, that counselors were the source of all his problems, etc. This in response to a girl's question of me: "What do I do if somebody tells me they're going to commit suicide?" I answered that you should try to get the person to a counselor. Chris told us about his two suicide attempts. Carla seemed disgusted by the conversation and stormed out of the room after the class. I think she is someone who has attempted suicide. The main source of passion, as it turned out, had to do with gun ownership, not suicide per se. Kyle was disgusted by my observation that if people insist on having guns, they ought to keep them locked up.

I begin by reporting that a girl has "asked me to talk about" this suicide incident, not that she has "asked if we can talk about it as a class." I do not remember now what the girl actually said. She may or may not have used the wording I report above. In either case, my reading of it makes me central to the emotional conversation, particularly juxtaposed with the line "I promised I would and I did." Yet my account depicts events as out of my control. So I am passionately central to these events but do not control them. While I was "quite uncomfortable" with the events, I report the fact by "including me" in the report that "everybody" was uncomfortable. Two of my students are "disgusted," I say; one storms out. Although I care, I cannot take responsibility. Instead, I sit there on the trackless trolley in wonder, and I acknowledge to myself—by objectifying for myself apart from the tangle of my feelings—how messy and unpredictable teaching often is in a moral as well as a practical sense.[3]

I think everyone who teaches has days like this. They serve as signs of the tentativeness of one's grip, the fragility of one's control. Such signs can be very useful, though they may also raise issues of control to excessive prominence. "The conversation let loose a torrent of strong feelings," I say uncomfortably. My discomfort is the stuff that often smothers authentic relations in teaching, turns classrooms cold and alien. The problem is that torrents of feeling, or torrents of anything, are not widely valued in teaching. Teachers are expected to be always in control. Yet, though I say that my students and I were made uncomfortable by this torrent, it is possible that we nonetheless learned a great deal by enduring it. Certainly I learned something by pausing to read it.

March 27

I was observed today by the principal. It went "well," which means (1) I got the kids who usually bring food to class to hide the food today, explaining that it was because the principal would be visiting; (2) that I didn't have the problem I'd had in the first-period class of having kids demonstrate quite plainly that they hadn't learned what I'd taught them—about refining a topic of interest into a researchable question; (3) that I didn't have to abandon plans I'd drawn up—as, of course, I had had to in the first period—in order to reteach, or teach something I hadn't expected to have to; (4) that my plans were able to be used almost exactly as I'd intended, that there was therefore no need to improvise; (5) that I "remembered" my plans without *too much* difficulty; (6) that there was none of the usual messiness of kids coming late, leaving early, of my getting started late, of kids distracting me from my purpose, of Don fooling around, of Shari challenging me and causing some scene, etc.; (7) that the kids were far more subdued than they are normally; (8) that I taught much more directly to an *objective* than I ever normally would have, and that I therefore evaded the messiness of accommodating kids' misunderstandings, that I actually taught today as if what I was saying was automatically sinking in (the fact that after class, Dan, who never listens to what I say but nonetheless does well in the course, came up to ask me something that showed clearly that he hadn't learned anything, was only a small embarrassment that the principal probably didn't notice); (9) that Tricia told me later—after I had congratulated her and others on how well they'd behaved, that she thought the class was boring, and that I admitted that it was far less lively than usual.

When the class ended, Reg picked up my handouts and papers for me as if he were my teacher's aide, and as if he sensed that I probably could use a hand picking up loose ends. He didn't say a thing about the class when we met later, though we talked for an hour about administrative things.

"Reg" of the second paragraph is, of course, "the principal" of the first. I would have ordinarily called him Reg throughout, except that in this first paragraph, I am striving to read something more abstract in the episode, some thought about teaching that transcends my own experience and reduces both Reg and me to types. Hence the irony, whose subtext, I think, is neither a complaint about the conditions of teachers' work nor a comment on the futility of observation. Nor is it unsympathetic toward Reg and his discharge of the observer's role. As "Reg," rather than "the principal," he instinctively helps me in the way that anyone who read my teaching sensitively would be drawn to help me—by tending to my loose ends, giving me a figurative dose of lecithin. If he fails to talk with me about the class, though we talk for an hour about other things, it may be because he also felt the lifelessness of my teaching earlier but wishes to signal me that this has not disturbed his confidence in me.

The subtext of the irony, as I read it, is that I am my own supervisor and that Reg and textuality are my supervising tools.[4] Prompted by Reg's silent visit, and from an ironic height, I see my teaching with a clarity otherwise unavailable to me. For example, I see the little treaty I've made with kids who bring food to class, one of possibly a hundred bargains I've made with my classes (Powell, Farrar, & Cohen, 1985; Sedlak, Wheeler, Pullin, & Cusick, 1986). Some of these treaties or bargains may be good from the point of view of learning, but some of them—like this one—are bad: Teaching a kid engrossed in a bagel dripping cream cheese is usually futile as long as the bagel lasts. The text displays this particular bargain in all its manifest indiscretion, a warning to me against deeper corruption.

The irony also enables me to see the limits of what we ordinarily call supervision. Throughout American elementary and secondary education, this more myopic supervision hinges upon such classroom

visits as Reg's. Its presumption is that it sees what *is*—in some impossibly objective sense. In fact, it sees a fabrication constructed more or
less delicately, or more or less clumsily, by all the parties to the experience, tailored to the dimensions of their collective sense of what is
supposed to be seen.

This sense is ideological. That is, it is governed by a system of
ideas that are deeply set and regarded more or less as "natural." In this
case, Reg, my students, and I all act in an ideologically correct manner, though we undercut the ideology, too. Reg makes the visit but
never talks to me about it. My students act their part but tell me later
that the result was boring. I act my part too, but view it from an ironic
distance later and question its worth. Our intuitive problem with the
ideology—which I will dub the ideology of effective teaching and
treat more fully in the next chapter—is that it imposes certainty where
uncertainty is more authentic. It seems to deny the proper place in
teaching of contingency and volatility. It has too many givens: that I
will teach as I've planned, that students will behave as predicted, that
they will learn what I intend. It has no respect for un-givens: a fire
drill, a bagel dripping cream cheese, the snit some student is in, the
hundred misunderstandings that might arise between teaching and
learning. These are all unseemly interruptions from the perspective of
effective teaching, not elements potentially equal in their effects to
any of the givens or guarantors of the lively against the boring.

My trolley reading of this moment of "supervised" teaching
brings me, by way of irony, to the very brink of disavowing inauthen-
tic certainty in teaching, though I cannot on this particular trolley ride
quite manage the plunge.

April 22

Difficult struggle with both classes today. The research papers
were due, but less than half came in. I'm frightened to think of
the condition of those, too. My teaching went well, but it was
hard to keep up courage given my disappointment over the papers. It's so easy to cave into the constant resistance from kids, so
easy to accommodate it. Also so personally wrenching to put on
the screws. Then there's the other test: how to insist not simply
on surface compliance but on genuine compliance, quality work.

[Later]

After writing the above, I had a chance to do some targeted
teaching, some tutoring of individuals based on a diagnosis of
what they specifically needed to learn. I took Martha through all

the steps of searching for a library source, got a close look at all
her difficulties in reading the card catalogue and the *Reader's
Guide,* etc. I was right with her as she stumbled and could see exactly how to help. Then I worked with Rachel on her first draft
and got to understand the problems she saw in it. It was so satisfy-
ing—in marked contrast to the impotence I sometimes feel in
teaching the whole class.

It reminded me vividly of the days when I used to work with
Mary. She was so good tutoring, so patient and perceptive in her
diagnoses, so exacting in her teaching to specific needs—but she
was no good at the inspirational, off-target, whole-group teaching
that I could do—no good at framing assignments, linking them up
with what's gone before, what will come later. But we were such
great partners. She needed me feeding her. But without her pull-
ing me closer to the reality at key moments, everything I did
would have been worth so much less.

The only time I've ever been able to teach like both Mary and
myself was when I had two-hour classes in summer school. In
two hours every day, I could reserve time to be both teacher and
tutor. So why the hell don't we do something about this stupid
design we have for high schools?

Facing up to uncertainty in teaching does not mean resigning oneself to ineffectuality. Quite the reverse can be true, as I think the
progression of these four paragraphs shows. In the first, I face up to
the fact that my teaching plan has not produced the results I expected.
It must have been a painful paragraph to write, because it contrasted,
no doubt, with what I admitted publicly to the kids. I probably kept
up my courage before them by projecting belief in my teaching and
their learning, perhaps concealing how many papers had actually
come in, or admitting it with righteous anger in my voice rather than
dejection. But I admit the dejection on paper—and immediately, too,
not even waiting for the trolley.

Then the second paragraph begins with the only sign in the entire
journal of a continued entry: "After writing the above . . . " It signifies a connection: I undertook the tutoring to fight off the dejection.
And it worked.

The third paragraph recalls a teaching arrangement I once enjoyed
with a colleague who was a reading teacher. I taught a writing class,
and she tutored a number of kids in the class who needed special help.
We also met weekly to plan common strategies, and sometimes we

visited each other's teaching, too—she joining the class, I overhearing or debriefing one of her tutorial sessions in our joint office.

Such arrangements are sadly and absurdly rare in teaching on any level, especially in high school. But why? The angry question erupts in the culminating fourth paragraph. Even if I can't work with a colleague, I imply, I can at least have enough time to alternate the two roles that I was able to play this day only by accident—maybe because Martha's and Rachel's fourth-period teacher happened to be absent, and I happened to be so bummed out as to need a different perspective even at the cost of giving up my coffee break. There are better ways to cope with all this uncertainty, I seem to say, than to pretend it away in little installments of time suitable only for pretending.

Of course, facing uncertainty does not by itself lead one to question structural norms. There are many hidden texts lurking behind the progression of these four paragraphs—I'd been doing a lot of reading other than of my own teaching. But I am convinced that facing uncertainty is an indispensable step toward a genuine questioning, without which all the things one might read about improving teaching and schooling cannot sink in. Nor should they. The true value of such readings is their power to inform practical directedness, to bolster one's effort to cope with uncertainty. Otherwise they just add more weight to the suppression of the teacher's voice.

As I knew only intuitively when I first read Scheffler's phrase, but as I knew more explicitly after keeping this journal, the teacher's voice is the thing we call the teacher's deep-set knowledge that knowing itself is unsure in teaching, that one can only take one's best shot. Dewey (1929) put it more elaborately: No matter how smart or skillful practitioners are, their "judgment and belief regarding actions to be performed can never attain more than a precarious probability" (p. 6). Still, as Heisenberg showed, that's enough.

4

Reading Over Pizza

The story begins with a reading assignment. In 1983, a group of teachers that called itself the Secondary Study Group invited Theodore Sizer to drop by one of its meetings in order to talk about the progress of his Study of the American High School.[1] In exchange, the group promised some pizza and committed itself to read any book he assigned. He assigned one of his favorites, Sarason's (1971) *The Culture of the School and the Problem of Change*.

I recall vividly my reaction then as a member of the group to this book that later became important to me: It seemed too theoretical. Nevertheless, I enjoyed our vigorous discussion with Sizer, who took off his jacket and rolled up his sleeves and seemed genuinely to enjoy the pizza and our concrete talk about teaching. It did not occur to me at the time that his enjoyment was as much professional as personal. Teachers are not used to thinking that they know some things that people who study schools find interesting and useful, anymore than they are used to serious discussions of theoretical texts.

One result of Sizer's visit was that our group acquired a reading habit, which in time came to involve the use of theoretical texts to gain a grip on our own experience of teaching. We also acquired a habit of inviting other researchers and authors to visit, though as far as I can recall we never again invited one to give us a reading assignment. We teachers quickly learned that we could teach ourselves, give ourselves our own reading assignments—that the occasional visitor could be merely a fresh and welcome voice at our own salon.

The Secondary Study Group began in 1982 as a result of a three-day conference sponsored by the Education Collaborative for Greater Boston and organized by two high school teachers, Paula Evans and Henry Bolter. The conference was funded by grants from the National Endowment for the Humanities and the Massachusetts Department of Education. It was action-oriented, aimed at fostering collaboration or collegiality across schools, specifically among the energetic and idealistic Boston-area high school teachers in attendance.

I believe that we who attended this conference were attracted to its vision of cross-school collegiality because we sensed that it might offer some protection for our energy and ideals in the face of changing times and our own aging. Most of us had begun our teaching careers in the late 1960s, eager to do good work and confident that our good work would be appreciated. In the years since, many of us had been innovators in one sense or another, often experimenting in the corners of an expansive system. But then, just as we were approaching mid-career, the early 1980s brought hard times: a conservative swing, fiscal austerity, program cutbacks, even layoffs. We decided to keep our conference going indefinitely, to keep talking with each other so that we might face these hard times together. So, the conference became a group, a monthly dinner club with an invariable menu in the first few years: pizza, beer or soft drinks, and a rambling but spirited conversation about schools and teaching in them.

We bonded—men and women—in our sometimes raucous pizza dinners, and in the process created a rare opportunity. This was the chance to talk with one another about our teaching absent the need to believe wholeheartedly in its efficacy. With no kids nearby, with no method or ideology at stake, with no particular school community to sustain through believing, and in the supportive company of our peers, we could put believing temporarily aside. In the earliest years of the group, our sense of the teacher's voice was simply this: the sound of teachers talking to each other after a long silence. I do not mean absolute silence; I mean silence about work and about the feelings, insights, and knowledge that arise at work. The reason our conversation was so rambling and spirited then, why we often struggled to get the floor, like sixth-graders waving arms for the teacher's call, was that we had a lot of silence to overcome.

PHASES IN THE GROUP'S DEVELOPMENT

The Secondary Study Group did not begin life as a reading group, but rather as a discussion group set about the task of breaking professional silence. It underwent an evolution, however, patterned after that undergone by many feminist groups and, Freire (1970) would suggest, by other groups who break a long silence. The pattern involves reading. We started just with talk, but soon more than talk was needed to deal with what talk stirred up. This lead to a first cycle of reading. However, we found that much of what we read seemed to exclude what we knew, and this angered us. Later, we learned to turn our reading upon our own experience in order to illuminate what we knew—which is to say, theorize about it. This involved writing, and a new, enriched cycle of reading.

Now I have gotten a bit ahead of the story. In the academic year following Sizer's visit, our group became a critical circle. It was the year the *Harvard Educational Review* dubbed "the year of the reports" ("Symposium on the Year of the Reports," 1984), and we decided to read and critique as many as possible of the reports and books about high schools that the year produced. We were hardly open-minded: We distrusted the ability of the theorists and polemicists who were writing these texts to get at the truth of high schools. They did not know what we knew; even we hardly knew what we knew.

The first "report" we tackled was Adler's (1982) *Paideia Proposal.* In preparation for our discussion of it, one group member, Marshall Cohen, committed some of his thoughts to paper and brought the paper with him to the group. After some of us read what he had written, we urged him to try to get it published. Some months later it appeared as the back-page essay of *Education Week* (Cohen, 1983). This was the first of what became a series of writings inspired by our reading. Thus the Secondary Study Group cultivated its voice to gain some say in policy. This was the point of Cohen's essay—to insist that any school board or principal about to take Mortimer Adler seriously take Marshall Cohen seriously, too. The group adopted a political aim to sit beside its psychological one—to transform the teacher's role from that of passive recipient of policy made to active participant in policy making. Nor did we think of our political voice as something to be given us, but rather something to be taken.

One other fruit of this phase in the group's development was the publication of a review of one of the major works of "the year of the reports"—Boyer's (1983) *High School.* Written by the group's co-founder, Paula Evans, the review is based on a transcribed conversation of the group, with occasional quotations included and the names and school affiliations of the parties to the conversation listed at the end (Evans, 1984). Interestingly, it is a rather scathing review of a book regarded by many as sympathetic to teachers. Evans told me that when she showed an early draft of the review to a friend who is a superintendent of schools, he urged her to soften its criticism in recognition of the fact that Boyer at least acknowledges the need to improve the working conditions of teachers. Why not reserve attacks, her friend suggested, for the reformers whose agendas view teachers as mere tools of those who make and enforce policy? But voiceless groups are particularly wary of those who would seem to support their achievement of voice while subtly undercutting it. "While he cites the need for teachers, parents, and students to become involved in developing their own school plans," the review says at one point, "his 'agenda for action' usurps their initiative by defining all the priorities and guidelines for change and urging the adoption of his proposals" (p. 366).

The fact is, our reaction to Boyer was as much epistemological as political. What gives Boyer the right to make recommendations about high schools? What does he really *know* about them? So, for example, the review comments on his knowledge of students:

> His description of students is almost always tied to some notion of their future opportunities or limitations. He divides students into two categories—those who will go on to some form of higher education and those who will go on to work. He seems hardly aware of high school students in the present. They are a complex, demanding lot. We found ourselves asking, "Has he met the beast?" (Evans, 1984, p. 366)

We had, of course, met "the beast," but we were still a few steps from inquiring into what the encounter meant, what we knew as a result of a career of encounters. We did not, for example, inquire into our own metaphor. Why "beast"? The story of the Secondary Study Group as a reading group is a story of how our reading habit grew so that we came to read ourselves—beastly metaphors and all. We started with textmaking—a conscious, even self-conscious effort to frame our experience. We learned, by fitful effort, to notice some of the contours of this experience. Finally, with the help of many other texts we read along the way, we learned to read deeply.

A READING EXPERIMENT

In its 1984–85 season, the Secondary Study Group undertook an experiment that lasted for only four sessions but permanently altered the group's reading style and purpose. The experiment was suggested by a member who argued at the end of one session that we stop reading books that cost too much and say too little. We're the experts, he said. Let's read us. We responded to his urging by deciding to depart for a while from our habit of reading outsiders' writing. We would instead prepare "teaching anecdotes" to share or read together.

In describing our experiment as anecdotal business, we at least intuitively confronted canons of educational research that distinguish what is *merely* anecdotal from what is generalizable and thus more truthful in the sense passed on from Plato—less encumbered, that is, by circumstance and contingency and details associated with practical life—in brief, more certain (Nussbaum, 1986; Schor, 1987).

Elizabeth's was one of the first anecdotes we read, and it established themes that continued throughout the experiment.[2] Rereading it now, in the grip of the anecdotes that followed it and in the grip of relevant theoretical texts, one may see that it deals with the role of interpersonal conflict in teaching and with the limits of caring and skill in ameliorating eruptions of conflict. It suggests that the teacher's own person, including in this case her social class, plays a mysterious but significant part in the configuration and resolution of conflict:

> I want to tell mine. . . . This was when Josh and I were doing a local history project with kids from Roxbury [a black neighborhood in Boston] and kids from Newton [a white suburb of Boston]. . . . We had planned this course very, very, very carefully—weeks of summer workshops—all of us—two people from the Boston high school, Josh and myself. We argued, we fought, we discussed what was appropriate and what wasn't appropriate for these two very different groups of kids, and we started the year out with a long, extensive unit on family and neighborhood history, in which the kids did a lot of sharing with each other about their family history, where they went to three different neighborhoods in Newton and three different neighborhoods in Boston and were led on tours by kids in the class through those different neighborhoods, and so on and so forth.
>
> This was a good two months into the course, and we were having what I thought was a really good discussion one day in Boston with just the Boston kids. I felt it was very important to structure the class carefully. These kids were truant a fair amount; and I had folders—I was using everything I knew—a folder on each kid; I was checking the homework every single day and they were getting it back the next day; if a kid didn't show up, I'd track the kid all over the building. I had time to do this. We were really on them. And I felt like it was a fairly cohesive group.
>
> We were discussing whatever the issue was—which I have blocked completely—but there was an argument going on between two kids. We were seated around the table like this, and

one kid was over there and one kid was over here. They were arguing back and forth, and there was some participation from the other kids, and Deborah, the other teacher, and I were sort of leading it and facilitating it, and there was five minutes left in the class, and, you know, I needed to talk about homework and one thing and another, and I said, you know, "Clearly we haven't finished this discussion, but we need to go on."

This one kid looked at me and he said, "I hate this class." He said, "I hate it. You never give us any answers in this class. Everything we ever discuss is always left unfinished. And I hate it."

And I said, "Wayne, Wayne, how can you say that?" This particular kid had a lot, he was very talented, and when we went on tours of neighborhoods, he could point out all the different architectural details. He knew the whole history of Roxbury. He was terrific. He couldn't write worth a damn. I was meeting with this kid twice a week to help him with his writing in addition to whatever. And he was telling me that he hated this class, and he was very angry. He was very angry at the kid across the way. I said, "We will finish it. There are lots of things that there aren't answers to."

I went on to give out the assignment because we had at this point two minutes left in the class, and all of a sudden I looked up and Wayne had walked around to the other side of the table and he and Chris were arm wrestling. And finally one of them won, and he looked up at me, and he said, "There, I feel much better."

The end of it is that the kid dropped the course at the halfway mark when kids had an option to stay in or go out. He said, "I don't like the kind of class that you have. I don't have other classes like this." He wasn't as articulate as I'm being about it, but he didn't like the kind of class, and I have had kids drop classes or tell me they didn't like classes for lots of different reasons, but never for that one. . . . You know, I had done all the familiar things that I was used to doing, and that had always worked.

The group members had listened attentively to Elizabeth and were now ready to respond.

ARTHUR: You prefaced all this by saying that you were really being Goody Two Shoes about this teaching stuff. I mean, you were really on top of everything. You were so good, that he could not abide you. So in control. I think that's often the problem that—I mean, I don't know whether you gave up and sort of messed up the details at all, and let the homework go for two days instead of one.

ELIZABETH: But I don't know. I mean, I felt that I was being quite myself with these kids. I mean, I was screaming at them. I was getting them in there and saying, you know, "You've got to do this work, and I want to see it," and making them do it over again. . . .

   But, let me just add one little sort of coda to this. They were nagging me at the Boston school all the time about how you're from Newton and you don't know, you don't know these kids, and so finally I said, "Yeah, give me a class, give me a regular U.S. History class." So they did, and my God! I prepared for that class for three weeks. I mean I did an enormous amount of research and stuff, because they were using a textbook that had been written for idiots, I mean, for people with IQs of 30 or below. It was so simple—no chapter was longer than two pages, and then there were all true-false, multiple choice. These kids were juniors; some of them were nineteen years old. I walked in and I had Xeroxed up these original documents, and I had this class straight for two weeks. It went fairly well. These kids were really into talking and stuff—they couldn't write at all, but they loved talking and they loved discussing. They fought the fact that we wouldn't do the textbook.

   But the third day into it, I'm just up there sweating, you know, I'm leading this discussion and I'm trying to pull kids in, making sure the radio's turned off in that corner and one thing and another, and this kid yells out—you know, I think things are going well—and this kid yells out, "Hey, are you a teacher?"

   I thought, What the hell is this? It was like I was a Studebaker.

RICHARD: Neither cat nor dog.

ELIZABETH: But I was trying to get these kids to sort of join me, and I realized I didn't know anything about it.

SUSAN: What did you say to the kid?

ELIZABETH: I said, "Yeah, I am." He said, "You teach here?" I said, "Yeah, I do." I didn't dare mention Newton at that point. He said, "You don't look like one."

RICHARD: Did you look like the other teachers, or was it something else?

ARTHUR: It was that Newton tweed.

ELIZABETH: Let me think about that. Yeah, in some ways, I probably did look different. . . . A lot of the teachers dressed up
much more than I. I didn't wear pants or anything like that.
You know, a skirt, a sweater, maybe boots—it was the middle
of winter.

In this urban school, where she is a suburban outsider, Elizabeth
believes in her work. She has high expectations for the students and is
angry at what she perceives to be the school's condescension toward
them. In particular, she has high expectations for Wayne, with whom
she spends extra time, but who "hates" her class in return. The hate
eludes the power of her expectations; it also eludes the power of her
knowledge. She had done everything she *knew* how to do. Despite it
all, Wayne senses that her difference, symbolized for him in the irreso-
lution of one discussion, is too much to bear. It is ironic that for
Wayne, Elizabeth's teaching founders on her portrayal of uncertainty
in the world—"there are lots of things that there aren't answers to."
This is surely not by itself a shocking thought for Wayne, but may be
in juxtaposition to Elizabeth's apparent certainty about her teaching
and about his potential learning.

As the "coda" reveals, their dispute is associated with social class.
The fabric of the teacher-student relationship is always constructed at
least partly of the teacher's self. She is "up there sweating," engaging,
pushing, even "screaming," being herself as she puts it—but this self,
wrapped in "Newton tweed," cannot quite pull it off. "I remember
sort of looking at myself," she says, seeing suddenly, in an epiphany, a
different self. In other circumstances—in Newton certainly—this self
could have pulled it off, could have benignly swallowed up the conflict that is generated whenever one human being engages, pushes,
screams at another—even in the other's interest. But in these different
circumstances, this self is alien, ineffectual, a "Studebaker." Elizabeth's remark, "I realized I didn't know anything about it," does not
refer to technical knowledge. The *it* here is not a technical problem
that Elizabeth could solve if only she could draw the right solution
from the bank of her knowledge. It is instead a moral problem that has
caught her and her students in a web. Within this web neither can act
in a wholly rational and instrumental fashion.

Arthur's comment, beginning "You prefaced all this by saying you
were really being Goody Two Shoes about this teaching stuff," is an
invitation to read in Elizabeth's anecdote signs of a pedagogical
knowledge that is contextual rather than instrumental. This is knowledge about the limits of technique, about the place of uncertainty in

practice, about all the webs—moral and otherwise—that catch teachers and their students.

What I have just claimed is, as I suggested earlier, the product of rereading Elizabeth's anecdote in the light of the anecdotes that came later and in the light of other, more theoretical texts. At time of telling, however, neither I nor any of our group noticed this much in her story. In fact, we hardly paused long enough between anecdotes that evening to notice anything at all. Still, one can feel, in the subtle thematic connections among the anecdotes, a growing power to notice what they contain. So Gretchen's story follows Elizabeth's.

GRETCHEN: My husband and I for our anniversary went to a Boston hotel—to get away for one night, and I called room service, and this kid answers—[*chuckles*] our night alone!—

SUSAN: Oh, no, I can't stand it!

GRETCHEN: And this kid says, "Gretchen?" . . . a kid whom I had four or five—must have been five years ago, and my memory of her is that I fought with her the entire year, that I was the one who was setting limits on her behavior where no one had . . . but I had an opportunity to get into a relationship with her because I was running an alternative program. . . . And this was a kid, I mean we argued should she or shouldn't she be in the program because she was heavily into alcohol and drugs and acting out . . . and probably a kid who in other schools would just have been booted, but we took her on. And I have to say that most of the time I wondered about our judgment. . . .

Anyway, she lived in the city and she had a job in a restaurant, which led to her eventually getting this job at the hotel . . . where she has worked her way up, and she's now in a hotel management training program. This is a kid who wouldn't have gotten out of high school easily. And she said, "I've got to come up and talk to you." I looked at my husband and said, "Will you forgive me?"

. . . My memory of this girl and her experience was very negative, and yet what she said is that it was a turning point in her life. She'd had a lot of ups and downs, but she was getting her life together. She thanked me for putting up with her, and that she knew she was difficult, and in retrospect she remembered things that I'd said to her that I can't remember saying at all—something like "Life is like a puzzle," that kind of stuff. [*Laughter*].

RICHARD: All those old chestnuts.
GRETCHEN: And I said, "Oh, yes, well . . . "
CARL: So it is.
SUSAN: And here are all the pieces getting together in your hotel
room.

Like Elizabeth's, Gretchen's anecdote highlights the mysterious territory of teaching that lies beyond intention. But while Elizabeth's anecdote offers a kind of photographic negative of this territory, Gretchen's offers the positive print. Elizabeth tries hard to teach something but fails; Gretchen teaches something inadvertently: "Life is a puzzle." As Carl and Susan note wittily, teaching is, too.

The anecdotes are complementary in another way also. Gretchen's, by means especially of its symbolic setting—a love retreat suddenly displaced by an old teaching commitment—gives perspective to the conflict that Elizabeth's story examines. Here the teacher remembers conflict, too, but the student remembers something else besides: a fidelity that over time managed to justify the conflict and in a sense supersede it. The term *fidelity*, as applied to teaching, comes from Noddings (1986), who intends it to denote a core practice of authentic teaching, whereby toughness and affection coexist, each in the light of the other.

The next anecdote, Catherine's, elaborates on this theme as it stretches the notion of anecdote to include the story of a unit or set of lessons she likes to teach. It also questions the common assumption that teaching must involve an exchange of knowledge, and it constructs a different role for the teacher from that of provider. Catherine begins by saying that she first undertook the design of her unit out of "desperation": She had a group of students whose needs for her caring seemed to outstrip what she could provide. She is in the habit of *providing* as she teaches, but she seems here to discover another way. Here little is provided, but much is enabled. Can this be teaching, too? Hal highlights the question by puzzling over Catherine's offhand remark that her work is not really work. Reading as an interpretive activity—an activity more complex than basic decoding—hinges on glitches like this, textual assertions that strike the reader as incongruous (Scholes, 1985). Why does Catherine say that this work is not work? What does she mean by *work*?

I thought I might mention a thing that I've done . . . that I started
doing really in desperation about seven years ago when I had a
class of kids that, you know, my stomach got tight on the week-

ends just thinking of them. . . . For me, it provides about six weeks of basically no lesson planning, incredible involvement on the part of the students, and it has always had the effect of making the class a unit. And so I thought I'd tell you what I do. It's a very simple idea. I do this between Thanksgiving and Christmas— you know, when nothing works. I ask kids over Thanksgiving to look at their families, to watch what happens on Thanksgiving and write about it, and that's all I say. I tell them that we're going to be looking at families for the next six to eight weeks, and I've kind of refined this more and more. . . .

Basically what happens is each kid gets half the class period to talk about his or her family, and that keeps us from one holiday to the next. And I have a lot of refinements added in, which I could talk to you about, but what happens is pretty incredible, because kids make connections with their own experiences and to each other that are very rare and special. I try to give them lots of tools to help them so they get some kind of control. I give them a lecture that presents five different frameworks. I won't bore you with them, but I have an example of one: I say that all families are both separated and connected.

Catherine goes on to talk a little about how these frameworks create questions, observational guideposts, lenses on experience. She also talks about a fairly elaborate integration of reading and writing assignments in the unit.

As I say, it was a very easy thing to teach. It totally took the focus off me. . . . The advantage of this kind of thing is that each kid feels better about their family at the end of it . . . because I think that kids during adolescence feel so locked into their families— everyone believes that they're the only one with money problems, alcohol, suicide, manic-depression, adoption, and each family has at least some of those stories, and kids do tell them. . . .

For us [teachers] . . . we seem to work incredibly hard, not always with great results. . . . Sometimes it really doesn't seem worth it, so I just wanted to tell you all that this is something that involves no work on my part. I mean, I walk in and it's not my class. . . . It feels wonderful to have kids be on the spot. Our kids—I don't know whether this is true of other people—but I feel that our kids have more needs and fewer skills and are more draining than they were ten years ago, and that somehow that this experience of having to put out for other people, having to reach out, and also having attention, I think, has continued to work.

Here Hal tries his interpretive bid, but only John responds.

> HAL: I don't know how you respond to Catherine's saying that this is not work, but I think of what she just told us as a tremendous demonstration of skill and of work, but not work of sitting home and making up a lesson.
> JOHN: On a day-to-day, class-to-class basis, there's a kind of skill that is sort of like good counseling—you don't prepare for it, but you have to have a lot of skills, you have to be there.

In the way she chooses to *be there,* Catherine manages the tension Elbow (1986) describes between the teacher's commitment to nurture and support students and her commitment to cherish the subtleties and standards of knowledge. Catherine's family unit is at once good counseling and serious intellectual activity—caring for students and also pushing them to think. Using it, Catherine achieves the tenuous balance that eludes Elizabeth and that Gretchen finds only in retrospect.

This problem of achieving balance and of dealing with the conflict that otherwise arises is prominent in all the anecdotes. One session, for example, featured a whole string of what the group called "horror stories," like Sarah's account of her experience as a young teacher losing control of a group of children on an overnight fieldtrip to northern New England. Among her problems was one boy who ran away and another who broke all the windows on one side of the lodge where they were staying:

> Oh, it was awful. Everything went wrong. . . . We just didn't know what to do. Even if you knew what to do, you didn't know what to do, because there were things that were totally out of control. We got the kid back; we found the kid I don't know how many hours later. That was the worst worry. . . . And the people who owned the lodge were really good about the windows. . . . They empathized with us.

This "horror story," closely read, points below the surface of the way we typically speak of teacher's knowledge. "Even if you knew what to do," Sarah says, "you didn't know what to do," echoing Elizabeth's line earlier about a kind of knowledge more elusive than

technical knowledge. The paradox is a key to unlocking a subterranean chamber of what is called the knowledge base of teaching. Stored
below the technical knowledge furnishing the ground floor are several
other kinds of knowledge. These include knowledge of pervasive uncertainty in teaching; knowledge of the sources of this uncertainty in
conflict and caring and the swirling contexts that sustain and sur-
round both; and knowledge of what one does when one is uncertain
about what to do.

All the anecdotes explore this basement knowledge, though none
in a more stunning fashion than Ruth's. Hers concerns a conflict that
erupts in her classroom when an assignment involving personal writing strikes one student as something more intimate than Ruth intends.
Yet Ruth cannot merely dismiss the student's assumption—for reasons
of subterranean ambiguity. In fact, the assignment, like much teaching, tries to swallow the difference between cold demands (as in
school assignment) and warm associations (as in personal writing).
Fudging such differences is typical in teaching, though it may be over-
looked by theorists. From the point of view merely of the ground
floor of teaching's knowledge base, one may read the vulnerability
that Ruth feels acutely throughout this episode as sheer irrationality,
and the beastly metaphor she lets slip at one point as mere pique. One
reads more from below the ground floor, where one can see, cast
across all rational issues involved, the shadow of teaching poised between coldness and warmth, struggle and vulnerability—where one
reads uncertainty.

> RUTH: I gave last fall an assignment for kids to keep a thought
>   journal, and they were to keep it for a whole semester as a
>   daily record, and then it reduced to three times a week—a
>   record of what they thought about. They weren't to keep dia-
>   ries of events, and they weren't to keep a whole lot of emo-
>   tional stuff—of course, they had to be woven into thoughts,
>   but I wasn't wanting to keep an emotional record. It could be
>   how zippers work or the nature of democracy—there were a
>   whole lot of things. And kids wrote wonderful, wonderful
>   things.
>
>   Then at the end of the year, kids wrote evaluations of my
>   course—what things I should keep and change, and 95% of
>   the kids were enormously enthusiastic about the thought
>   journals, and one girl freaked out on me. She was really angry
>   that I knew more about her than she knew about me, and her
>   solution was—and this took two days to work out in class—

she thought that I should have passed out my journal to all 46 of my kids.

I thought to myself, I know what this argument is: This is an argument that says I don't like that you're the adult and I'm the kid. That's the problem here. And there was no way I could say, "Danielle, sorry, I'm the adult and you're the kid. That's how this works. There's no getting around that. We're not peers here." And part of my problem in fighting back was that with adolescents, you can't fight back fair. You have to be so fair to them that you're not fair to yourself.

SARAH: I'm curious to know what she wrote in her thought journal.

RUTH: That was part of the problem. She had written all year long very, very emotional stuff. I had suggested repeatedly, "Danielle, you don't want me to read all this stuff. Get two journals. I'll buy you a second one." I gave her a second one. "Put the emotional stuff in here, and give me ideas. Can you get these two separate?" So she's angry at the very thing that I've worked all year to get her to stop doing.

This escalates a couple of weeks later to bringing her mother in to talk to me about this because her mother wants to know about this journal reading. And it occurred to me when I was talking to her mother that her mother is saying everything the kid said.

I really went under on this. I felt so attacked on something that I felt like I had given and given and given.

STEVE: Yet 95% of the kids thought that this was great. Only 5% shot you down.

RUTH: Yeah, that feeling that the one kid who complains in class can undermine you totally. How many times this has happened in my life—when kids have been enormously supportive and appreciative, and even verbal about it—been grateful—I mean, not the nature of the beast. And then one kid complains.

I had visions of never going back to this class. I was trying to figure out how I could claim I had car trouble every morning—there were only so many days before summer vacation. I had all these fantasies about never going back to them. I know that I was in a fairly weak—not neurotic—but pretty vulnerable place, and that my reaction was way overreaction. I really didn't want to go back; I'm not exaggerating. I cried and cried about it.

BARBARA: She sounds like a powerful kid.

HAL: But so much of teaching is that vulnerability.

CATHERINE: I guess if you care a lot about what you've been doing, and you've been putting yourself out, you can be vulnerable to a pretty irrational degree.

STEVE: You've just got to grit your teeth and try to keep your sensibilities.

CRITICAL READING

The anecdotal experiment ran its course but yielded a long-term
benefit. For several sessions, we had self-consciously raised our voices, offered one another deliberately constructed texts about teaching.
And in discussing them, however briefly, we had taken a second step
in reading teaching: to notice its quirky details and puzzle over them.
When, after the experiment, we returned to reading other texts and to
more desultory conversation about our own experience, we were
ready to take the third step, toward critical reading. I mean this in the
sense described in Chapter 2. Critical reading holds a teaching text in
the temporary grip of another interest—one that is inherent in another
text or another perspective. The grip enables the reader to notice deep
structures that might otherwise escape notice (Scholes, 1985).

The following conversation took place in May 1985. The meeting's assigned reading was an essay about his teaching by group member Donald W. Thomas (Don to the group). Entitled "The Torpedo's
Touch," the essay was later published by the *Harvard Educational
Review* (Thomas, 1985) as the first of a distinguished series of essays
by teachers on teaching. It describes Thomas's first teaching experience, as a student teacher assigned to teach Jonathan Edwards's "Sinners in the Hands of an Angry God." The young Thomas taught this
sermon by delivering it himself, after having darkened the classroom,
having asked his students to raise their desktops in imitation of the
Puritans' high pews, and having climbed a pulpit built by piling a
lectern on top of his desk. From this height, wearing his jacket reversed, Thomas spewed Edwards's fire and brimstone on his seventh-
graders.

In the essay, Thomas recalls their reactions to the lesson: They
"sat gaping and transfixed in their pews." The lesson had been "stunning." Meanwhile, his supervisors, apparently stunned in a somewhat
different way, "madly" scribbled critiques in the back pew (p. 220).

They were relentless in their queries. What had been my objectives? What had the children learned? How did I propose to measure this learning objectively? . . . What skills had the students employed and what had been my strategy for reinforcing them? Was I aware that I had used *slang*? (p. 220)

Exasperated by the assault, the novice teacher accepted defeat, but with a petulant retort: "I don't know what they learned, but they'll never forget it" (p. 221).

Thomas's essay may be said at least partly to be about how petulance prefigured wisdom in this case. It was in reading Plato's *Meno*— presumably some years after his teaching debut—that Thomas first discovered his "vindication" (p. 221). There Socrates compares himself to a certain fish, the torpedo, which stuns its prey. Socrates' stunning, or "torpifying," touch is the assault of "dissonance and perplexity," a teacher's willingness to be ungentle with students in the interests of their learning, to provoke their sense of their own ignorance even in the absence of any means of allaying it (p. 222). This was the logic, Thomas writes, that governed the impulse he felt as a young teacher to leap upon his desk and rain down Puritan determinism on the heads of his seventh graders. Today, while he no longer leaps upon desks—though "more's the pity," he writes (p. 221)—he still tries to "torpify" every class he teaches:

Each time I enter class I bring with me some part of the abyss that I plan to reveal. We begin, as Socrates so often does, with pleasantries and talk of surface things. And as they negotiate these waters, splashing amiably about in specifics, I lie in wait for them, ready to deliver the torpedo's touch and pull them under as far as they can go. (p. 222)

On this May evening, we also begin with pleasantries and talk of surface things. The group always begins its sessions this way: gossip to start, discourse to follow. "People discourse *to* one another," Spacks (1982) claims, "they gossip *with*"; discourse takes place from a height, gossip around a kitchen table (p. 24). The point of the group's gossip is to make a connection among those present, so that the voice and the vision that are meant to follow (involving, as they must, disconnecting gestures such as making distinctions, pointing out contradictions, disagreeing, and so on) may have sufficient trust to develop.

So before we talk about Don's essay, we talk about other things.

Has anyone heard from George since he retired? Will he still come to the group? What is Chuck up to? Is he still feeling uncomfortable about teaching again after being away from it for some time? Sarah tells about a project that Margaret, absent tonight, has undertaken—an exchange of letters with a former student, one destined to be a future reading and the group's most celebrated publication (Metzger & Fox, 1986).

Although it is not gossip, according to Spacks's definition, there is also quite a bit of talk about the group itself, its past, my habit of taping it, how nonmembers view it, what might become of it, and so forth. As gossip can be also, this is self-affirming talk. It serves to move the group toward discourse, confident in its right and capacity to speak from a height. Then Catherine, in a mock serious tone, signals the switch: "Well, are we going to talk about this article, or are we going to talk about our group, or what? I need an agenda."

Elizabeth first considers Don's essay as an anecdote of experience—a primary text. Later, she will turn it into a gripping text, a means of gaining a critical perspective on another teaching story.

> ELIZABETH: This was your very first class? I just can't believe that
>   you had the nerve to do something like that.
> DON: How else are you going to do Jonathan Edwards?
> ELIZABETH: I don't know. I would've gotten up there and written
>   a lot on the board—I don't know—with all these people sit-
>   ting in the back of the room?
> DON: I didn't know they were going to be there.

In this first interchange, two themes emerge: admiration for Don's boldness and acknowledgment that he broke faith with a prevailing ideology. Although this is not yet apparent, both the boldness and the break of faith have as much to do with Don's ideas of teaching as they do with his Jonathan Edwards enactment. Trying to reconcile the themes, Elizabeth later torpifies herself. Meanwhile, Sarah, asking why he would choose to write now about his very first lesson, prompts Don to put Jonathan Edwards into a larger context.

> That's really what I sort of do when I go into a class. I go in with
> the notion that I will just play around, and just wait for them, you
> see? Start asking them questions—in the levels, you know? That's
> just the whole structure of the way I teach. Then, when I get
> them down far enough—and they love that—then I'll let them go.
> That's the whole trick, it seems to me—to find that thing, that lit-

tle thing, that you can use to open the whole—it's like a draw-
string.

So he recalls the torpedo imagery, with its implicit violence, its
trickery, its beastly referent. But here there is the tempering line:
"Then, when I get them down far enough—and they love that—then
I'll let them go." Violence plus love, constraint plus freedom—all
below the surface of what is commonly regarded as teaching technique, "down far enough."

John and Catherine put Don on the spot. The connectedness within the group—product of time together plus gossip—makes criticism
possible. John is unsure that the Jonathan Edwards enactment is "defensible" teaching. Don remembers that it was utterly indefensible in
its own time, that the behaviorist paradigm evident in his supervisors'
questions and universal in the teaching world then, as he recalls it,
had no room whatsoever for such teaching. He deflects another explicit part of John's question, though—about its defensibility today.
Catherine raises the issue in another guise—by questioning the relationship between the Jonathan Edwards lesson and what she considers Socratic teaching.

> CATHERINE: I feel this first incident, the dramatization, is totally
> not Socratic—no discussion, just experience, wham. . . . May-
> be your ultimate purpose was in the light of the next day's dis-
> cussion where you talked about it—but to me you just gave
> them an experience and you left it at that. It was to present—
> it wasn't to confuse. It was just to have an experience, some-
> thing unforgettable—which I see as something very different
> from discussing or having them argue or think about.
>
> ELIZABETH: I don't necessarily. I mean, it was a presentation, but I
> see it as a presentation which probably provoked endless
> numbers of questions and feeling, and all kinds of thoughts
> about this person and this situation.
>
> CATHERINE: Except that the whole thing takes place in the kid's
> mind when you're not there.
>
> HAL: But that doesn't mean that it's not happening.

Several key ideas about teaching surface in this snippet of conversation, all elements of a prevailing ideology of teaching. One is the
idea that good teaching is more definitively purposeful than Don's
seems. "Maybe your ultimate purpose was in the light of the next
day's discussion," Catherine says by way of softening what comes

next: "but to me you just gave them an experience and you left it at that." Her discomfort with what she takes to be Don's vagueness of purpose is rooted in a concept of teaching as a rational activity, the application of solutions to identified problems.

A second idea is that there is a necessary and discernible connection between teaching and its effects. "I don't know what they learned," claims Don to his supervisors, "but they'll never forget it." Absent any evidence of effects, if "the whole thing takes place in the kid's mind when you're not there," Catherine counters, can you be said to be teaching at all?

A third idea is that good teaching must be interactive. To torpify and suffer torpification hardly seems interactive. Elizabeth wants to like Don's Jonathan Edwards lesson and defends it in the face of Catherine's criticism; but she wants to save the idea, too, of the link between interaction and good teaching. That is why she suggests that the lesson was interactive in disguise.

Ironically, these ideas all have roots in John Dewey, who besides urging a proper regard for the uncertainty of practice, also urged a scientific view of teaching, and a pedagogy of interaction designed to merge means and ends (Archambault, 1964). Weakly reconciled even in Dewey's writings, these various urgings have tended to suffer different fates. The idea of uncertainty, as I have suggested, has largely been neglected. The scientific view of teaching and pedagogy of interaction, however, are powerful currents in mainstream thinking about teaching. They are joined by other distinctly non-Deweyan ideas in a grand coalition of prevailing ideology that we might call the ideology of effective teaching. One of the non-Deweyan ideas is the tendency to see teaching as the provision of knowledge. You may remember this as the ideological culprit behind Catherine's reluctance to define her family teaching as work (it hardly seems coincidental that she is a key participant in the dialogue here). Another is the behaviorist legacy: "We may argue," Don asserts in his essay by way of defining this legacy, "that the young need not be torpified, but on the contrary require clarity, structure, simplification, reward" (Thomas, 1985, p. 222). So we have at least the following currents in the ideology: that teaching is rational, that it is properly interactive, that it provides knowledge, that it involves primarily the manipulation of behavior. And we do not have another: that teaching is inescapably full of uncertainty.

Several things about torpification grate against this ideology. First is its metaphorical beastliness, the implication that teaching can be in some sense cruel and still be teaching. A second is its apparent capriciousness, its disdain for objectives and planning. A third is its assumption that teaching may fail to provide any*thing,* and still be teaching. As these points of conflict arise in the rest of the conversation, Don encourages the group to see them. He pushes for a critical reading.

> SARAH: Don, here was your first experience, and you knew the answer was "I don't know what it is that they learned, but I knew they learned something," as if it didn't matter about all the years of experience—you knew that answer back then.
>
> DON: But I didn't know that I knew it. It was just raw instinct, and I came out of there thinking that it was wrong instinct.
>
> ELIZABETH: You can't come in and do this kind of dramatic lesson every day, but you can come in every day with the expectation that you are going to play out what you talk about doing—leave people with questions, confuse them with their own thoughts.
>
> DON: But it's not in lesson plans. It just happens.
>
> ELIZABETH: But it's an understanding about teaching and learning, and about a relationship between you and those kids and some subject matter.

Now comes the introduction of another text: an anecdote about teaching offered by Elizabeth. Note how she begins—as if in struggling to read what seem to her contradictory messages, she has torpified herself.

> I'm perplexed. I just came from a class. This morning I went to a class with absolutely super, bright—these are all honors kids. This is in a suburban, very wealthy community . . . where they were doing *The Merchant of Venice,* and the teacher talked for the entire time that I was there. I sat for 30 minutes, and when he turned on the recording, I left. He talked for the entire time and quoted passages from *The Merchant of Venice,* and the only time he asked questions of kids, there were four responses—four, total. No response was longer than three words. He would say, "And for the quiz tomorrow, I'd like you to be able to distinguish between the three chests, and I'd like you to quote the marking on each chest. . . . " And he'd say one word, and some girl would say one word, and then he'd finish it for her, and that was the class.

Before proceeding with Elizabeth's statement of what has perplexed her, let's pause to read this new text closely. What details does the text provide about the teaching episode to which it refers?

First, the kids are "super, bright, suburban, very wealthy." The words are deeply coded. They have antonyms, which may be strung together as these are, but on the other side of a gash across American schooling: *basic, dull, urban, poor*. The gash is racial, class-based, and related to a particular theory of intelligence and of the function of schools. On one side of the gash, it is presumed that teachers can and will push hard, expect participation, get results; on the other side, it is presumed that these things are more problematic, less likely, more dependent upon heroism. Elizabeth, beginning in this coded way, merely means to say that the teacher need not have been a hero in order to do good work, because these were *good* kids. But, beginning in this way, she also reveals the pervasiveness of ideology. This may have piqued some group members' ideological scrutiny not only of the good kid/bad kid distinction, but of another distinction, more central to her remarks, namely good teacher/bad teacher.

Next detail: The teacher's text is *The Merchant of Venice*. In teacher code, this means tough text, because (1) it's Shakespeare, and (2) it's anti-Semitic. So, good kids, tough text. What can the teacher do? Among the teachers present for this conversation, a dozen answers doubtlessly spring to mind. Elizabeth assumes, probably correctly, that none of them involves talking "for the entire time." That phrase is code for bad teaching. Like the code for bad kids, it has ideological roots. So: good kids, tough text, bad teacher. Why was he bad? He asked inadequate questions, promised a trivially focused quiz, put words into his students' mouths. In short, he fit certain key dimensions of the prototype of bad teacher provided by the ideology of effective teaching. "And that was the class."

But of course *that* was not the class. That was the text representing Elizabeth's reaction as a visitor to the class, and embedded within it are assumptions that can be read critically. In what follows, it is read within the group in juxtaposition to Don's text and to a second textual fragment that drops in later. The reading provokes a series of questions and insights concerning teaching and represents, I think, a good and full example of reading teaching. One set of questions and insights concerns what teachers need to teach well and whether teachers can change how they teach. Another is about the function of control in teaching and about what is controlled. Another is about what teaching is. These sets of questions and insights play across the conversation without reaching the kind of resolution common in other kinds of discourse, and surely without allaying Elizabeth's perplexity. As Don might have said, though, sometimes the point of reading is to heighten perplexity.

Elizabeth's expression of her perplexity focuses on why "there aren't more people in teaching who think about teaching in some other way." Why does the teacher teach "badly"? Sarah responds with the first half of a nature/nurture argument. Elizabeth counters, and the argument goes on for some time.

SARAH: They don't have the personality.

ELIZABETH: So it's crazy Don, with an idiosyncratic personality over there, who thinks about teaching like this? It seems to me that all the people in this room think about teaching in similar ways—I mean, see it as a very complex—levels—makes me think of that dessert, what is it? Trifle. With lots of levels, each one being different, that you can't necessarily measure out and test and distill. . . .

Meanwhile, in disputing Sarah's answer, Elizabeth puts Don squarely on the side of the good teachers. Later, he provocatively walks back across the line.

SARAH: But the thing is, that teacher probably thinks the way he's teaching is right on target.

ELIZABETH: I understand that. I'm sure he does. He was very articulate—he said to me, "This is a great group of kids, they're very bright, they're very motivated, they'll read anything."

BARBARA: Maybe it has something to do with control.

ELIZABETH: God, these kids, Barbara, they were all beautiful kids.

BARBARA: Yeah, I don't mean controlling behavior, but—oh, I don't know . . . [*struggling to find words*].

SARAH: How controlling you are with your personality, and how much you can sort of free yourself up?

BARBARA: I think that teaching and learning—there's an element of magic to it. I don't want to use that word in a trite way. I mean, it's out of control. You don't know what you teach kids every time.

SARAH: There's a spontaneity.

BARBARA: Yeah, and you need to be someone who thinks a lot about teaching and learning and the magic part of it.

HAL: There's great danger in that, personal dangers.

BARBARA: It's risky, and there are dangers, because if you feel you can control the information that kids are getting, and that then you can measure it—then, if you let a class go, they might learn stuff you don't want them to learn.

ELIZABETH: What? Asking questions that you can't answer?

BARBARA: Right . . . and you might have to be engaged yourself in the process, and be out of control. Sometimes in my discussions with my seventh graders, I don't know what I think anymore. You know, the kids say stuff, and I say, "Hm, that's really interesting, I never thought of that." And that's risky unless you really trust yourself . . . and trust the situation you've set up. I don't know what I'm trying to say, I need to think about it more. But it feels like a control issue.

Is teaching like shooting, a matter of staying "right on target"? Or is another kind of incendiary image more appropriate—the magician's puff of smoke, sign of a transformation? Jackson (1986) distinguishes between "mimetic" teaching, which might be said to be *aimed* at the transfer of behaviors or concepts, and "transformative" teaching, which designs a kind of conversion experience. Control is an issue in either case, but control of what? Behavior? Information? Oneself? Or all of these, plus more? Catherine's remarks illustrate the problem:

I'm just thinking about the nature of the subject. I'm sure he's not that controlling when he teaches *Brave New World*. I'm teaching Shakespeare now, and there's something—for one who feels so familiar to it after you've done it for awhile—and it's so alien to the kids—that sometimes I think after that kind of class where they're totally discombobulated by it, I think that probably I should have—I mean, I come in with very sophisticated ideas—you know, like about the relationships between the three main characters in *Othello*—and sometimes I think I should have just *done* it, I should have just *done* it.

Done what? Given up some control? Or seized more? The ambiguity of her remark may reflect Catherine's ambivalence, which may in turn be related to the uncertainty she feels—as revealed earlier in her anecdote—about the place of provision in teaching.

DON: You have to have a certain tolerance for incompleteness, and I think that's particularly true of Shakespeare, if you do any of these plays. You know, just from what has taken place in class, they haven't got *it*. Right?

HAL: There's this metamodel of teaching—this idea of the commodity that comes from on high and is parceled down, and the teacher is the vehicle by which it's parceled down. It's what the teacher fears losing control of—that delivery process.

SARAH: For many people, like this guy who's teaching *The Merchant of Venice,* he just wouldn't be capable of doing it any other way. . . . I think that a lot of what goes into teaching is . . . just something that comes with you, part of your personality, the way you function, the way you behave—which is very different for all kinds of people, and there are people who are much more rigid and controlling, and who couldn't do it any other way—they just can't, they simply can't.

CARL: It seems to me that it has as much to do with people's vision of what's going on as it does with their personality. It seems to me that what we've been talking about is some sense of what we get up in the morning for. I'm thinking now about my own American History class—what I want them to have is some feeling about American history—to go away, and when they're 38 years old, wonder why something is done the way it's done and what the past of it was. In Shakespeare, you want some taste of Shakespeare, some feeling that there's life there, something that Shakespeare is saying to you—so you try all your tricks, but you're trying to beam out to the kids in various ways that message—and so there really is some vision involved.

CATHERINE: But whether the key is instinct, or as Sarah says, personality, or whether it's vision, can you monkey with it? Can you change it? Or is it a fixed thing? Is it something that people begin their career with, and then embellish or not? Is it an art like dancing that maybe you get better at? And, like dancing, is the relevant thing how much talent you start with?

CARL: Oh, I think, the answer is that you work at it and get better.

SARAH: But I still think—let's use that same teacher—what if he were to sit here with us and talk about what he wanted to see come out of his lesson? He might describe a vision that we would even agree to. I still think that he may not be capable of doing something different to get there.

Now, in drops a textual fragment.

HAL: I was going to say something else besides vision—something else that I think is necessary, and perhaps missing in *The Merchant of Venice* person. I was preparing a report on a conference about teaching with computers, and so I was listening to the tape of a teacher who spoke at the conference, describing an idea he had to use a certain piece of software. The software had a sort of moving chevron on the screen, and by keying in certain commands, you could make it go in certain ways—it mimics in certain ways, he thought, a frictionless environment. So at the same moment that he got the idea to use this software, he also connected it to space travel, and a whole unit tumbled out. He thought I'll show them a film about Sally Ride, the astronaut—this was a second-grade class.

In describing how the lesson all came together, he said, "In my mind, I had to make a connection between this software and space travel." Now I became convinced as I listened to it on the tape that this phrase, "in my mind," was not just a figure of speech. He really did literally mean that in his mind he had to be alive to the connection if the kids were ever going to be alive to the connection—that in other words, it couldn't be an abstract piece of curriculum or a lesson plan—that he had to be intimately excited about it for it to work.

BARBARA: It says something about while you're teaching, you're willing to be learning, too. That's what I meant when I said sometimes I don't know what I think anymore when I listen to the kids. And to be ready to go with that: to let the kids see that they sparked something in me, and I was now learning with them—that I asked the question back—that I'm an adult and a better reader or whatever, and so I can manage both at once—the teaching and the learning. That's like *The Merchant of Venice* story—what did that guy learn there?

ELIZABETH: He knows it cold.

HAL: Cold is the word.

Now Don takes his step back across the line, daring to trample on a sacred element of the effective teaching ideology—preparedness. He begins with a rhetorical question.

DON: When you go into the class, do you have a set of discussion questions? See, I don't. I don't have any questions. I don't know what I'm going to ask.

ELIZABETH: And they put a student teacher with you? [*Laughter*]

DON: Yeah, and I really felt I ought to be honest about it. I'll never get another one. I tried to tell her this.

SARAH: So are you telling us that you just read the material?

DON: Well, I think what Hal said makes it make sense—I have to get inside it. So what I have to do is I have to have, first of all, about ten minutes of silence before I go into the class—and I don't even know what I'm thinking about. I don't know what it is. And then I have to have a chance to read the passage and get myself inside it, and then I walk in and I don't have the faintest idea.

BARBARA: You have ten minutes before the class? [*Laughter*]

DON: Well, this is A block. It starts about eight o'clock, I get there about seven o'clock, so. For later classes, I take five minutes.

The conversation stops here—abruptly, as if the bell had rung to signal the end of the period. It is not that the tape ran out, but that amid Don's talk about time and 7:00 A.M. commitments, someone noticed how late the evening had grown and suggested adjournment. She might have noticed, too, that the conversation threatened here to take a major turn, poised at the crucial juncture of craft and school structure. If we let it make the turn, we might all have thought in an instant, we'll never get home tonight. So, time is the culprit twice over, stealing from Don's thinking, choking off our reading.

No matter—one cannot read everything in one evening, and when it comes to the connections and contradictions between teaching as an uncertain craft and the structure of schooling, there is much to read, including the following chapter.

5

Reading in School

The school reform movement, whose first gestures haunted my teaching in the trolley journal days, and stirred resentment in the early conversations of the Secondary Study Group, took an interesting turn later on. One can see the turn by comparing two of the movement's key texts: *A Nation at Risk* (National Commission on Excellence in Education, 1983) and *A Nation Prepared* (Carnegie Forum on Education and the Economy, 1986). Below rhetorical similarities built upon images of economic peril, one finds in these texts a startling difference: Whereas the earlier report implicitly takes teachers to be the dumb instruments of school policy, the later one takes them to be its chief agents. Of course, a school reform movement is not literally a "movement," nor does it "turn," but these metaphors capture the power and variability of a great public policy debate. Caught up in the 1980s debate about schooling in America, I first felt devalued as a teacher, then revalued, finally overvalued. In 1986, I did what the overvalued often do—I became a consultant.

I took on the task of trying to help a high school reform itself "from the bottom up." I will call it Bright High School.[1] The teachers there had themselves been recently revalued in a system in which they had formerly been thought the merest cogs. The shift of value was in this case encouraged by a hefty foundation grant, which paid for me, among other things. Just before I went to work at Bright, a university professor told me that she figured my consulting would involve a lot of "modeling" of good teaching. This is what I mean when I say I had been overvalued: She, among others, had an inflated sense of my craft's capacity for influence. This is what happens to "tokens," people presumed to embody in a nonthreatening way what some group finds otherwise very threatening: The token suffers a flattery that is fundamentally demeaning because it overlooks real value.

I knew that one cannot model teaching outside the triangle defined by an actual responsibility to teach something to somebody. Consultants can be helpful, I thought, but not helpful as models. And even if I had had my own classes to teach at Bright, I knew that the Bright teachers were not on the lookout for models who might be teaching down the hall. As teachers often do in troubled schools, most had largely retreated from common space. Many had strung curtains across the windows of their classroom doors. Few seemed to have enough confidence left either in themselves or in their students to notice their own teaching anymore, let alone another's.

On the other hand, a small group of veteran Bright teachers had volunteered to begin reversing this isolation and despair. They wanted to build a new Bright High School inspired by and affiliated with Theodore Sizer's Coalition of Essential Schools. They, too, were skeptical of models. In fact, they were attracted to the Coalition partly because it avoids modeling school structures the way I avoid modeling good teaching, and for the same reason: Local construction better fits local conditions. Instead of models, the Coalition offers its member schools a prestigious association that one might call construction insurance, plus a large scaffold in the form of nine principles (Houston, 1988; Sizer, 1989). These principles, agreed to by each member school as a condition of membership, propose a series of substitutions. The curriculum is to shift from attempts to be comprehensive toward a focus on essential intellectual questions. Students are to be active learners rather than passive receivers of instruction. Award of diplomas is to be on the basis of an exhibition of knowledge rather than an accumulation of credits. And students are to face a single set of high expectations, rather than expectations that vary by the students' social class and their presumed abilities and future careers. Taken together, these principles signify a radical transformation of the American high school—not just structurally, but in terms of its mission, attitude, and habits.

The principles are vague in that they do not specify essential questions, advocate particular teaching methods, or suggest specific policies and structures. In fact, they are typically expressed in common Coalition parlance by still vaguer, nearly Zen aphorisms: "less is more," "student as worker." Set against each other, two of the nine principles even seem contradictory: On the one hand, a school's goals should apply to all students; on the other hand, teaching and learning should be personalized. The vagueness and paradoxical quality of the principles constitute in themselves a tenth, unspoken principle. It is an acknowledgment that school change, like school itself, is full of ineluctable uncertainty; and that this uncertainty can only be handled in the local present, crafted into something else by means of vision, skill, luck, and principled believing.

So, refusing to be a model, what could I offer as consultant to this group of teachers and to the larger faculty that had launched their mission? What did I know? The question is the key question of the last two chapters, and the answer is the same, though it only dawned on me slowly. I knew something about uncertainty, and I also knew something about constructing provisional ways around it.

As it turned out, what I actually did as a consultant over the course of the next several years often involved storytelling. I took to storytelling for the same reason that the Secondary Study Group took to it, because stories preserve uncertainty, whereas many other kinds of discourse—such as theorizing, analyzing, and evaluating—often try to dispel it. At the same time, storytelling confronts uncertainty, too. It makes a structural commitment, defies the ineffability of experience by simplifying its terms and abridging its complexity. It believes in itself. The difference, however, is that the way it does these things often highlights ambiguities and dilemmas, and preserves them for later mulling over.

In becoming storytelling consultant to this high school, it was not as if I assumed a priestly role. I merely joined in a major institutional activity, albeit from an outsider's perspective. School is full of stories. Some are impossibly simple, some exquisitely complex. Some overlap and intersect with others. Some never do. The tacit aim of most school stories is to get a grip on a chaotically energetic world—to impose an order of which the constituent elements are perspective, conflict, climax, resolution, and continuity. Both teachers and students tell stories about school and their lives in school. Part of the task of teaching is to achieve sufficient congruence among these stories such that the storytellers, despite all the conflicts within and among their accounts, may perceive in them some large common complication, a nearly predictable denouement, a theme. Part of the work of administering a school is engineering the construction of a story that aims to integrate the school's great variety of perspectives and carry its energies through the tangled middle of its giant narrative.

As consultant storyteller, I often used stories to frame problems, to provide the teachers I worked with a kind of narrative arena within which to address common concerns. I learned, however, that such arenas had to be built from story material the teachers themselves supplied, that I could not invent my own material (Lighthall, 1989). My stories had to resonate with theirs, otherwise they were just an alien's alien stories.

Of course, I became a consultant reader of stories as well as a teller of them. I wandered the building searching for stories, finding many of them in the encounters that Hall and Hord (1987) call "one-legged conferences" to suggest the casualness of a leg crossed or propped up against a wall. The point of my casualness was not to mask a purposeful intervention, as if I were a secret agent, but rather to situate the intervention within daily life. And the point of the intervention was not to cajole or otherwise manipulate the ones encountered, but rather to provide them some bit of psychic space, protected for a moment from the rush of institutional life, wherein they might construct their own insights. So I would meet someone walking down a hall, washing up in the men's room, or standing in line in the cafeteria. I'd ask simply, "How's it going?" and a story might come my way. I might simply listen, or I might encourage a critical reading of this story by holding it to the light of some other story or bit of text. For example, hearing the often repeated story of the once proud Bright High School whose long decline commenced with desegregation, I might mention the alternative history told me once by a black teacher who had taught in the school during the years immediately following desegregation. She described a school full of growth and promise, turning upward not downward. I would offer this alternative history not as a point of debate, but as a point of critical reference.

One difference between writing and reading has to do with the precedence each gives to either believing or doubting. The great reductiveness of textuality cannot occur if believing does not take the edge in writing or, in this case, storytelling, nor be beneficial if doubting does not take the edge in reading (Elbow, 1986). I believe that this is so regardless of whether the texts involve teaching, consulting, or research. In all three cases, by means of the complex process of their construction, texts become necessarily and usefully invested with belief, which is also necessarily reductive or hyperbolic. All three demand critical reading—reading that deconstructs, gives doubt the edge. The point, at least as I practice such deconstruction, is not to deny ultimate value, nor to disparage truth seeking, nor, certainly, to devalue teaching, consulting, and research. The point is to balance yearning for certainty with practical awareness of contingency, ambiguity, volatility; to acknowledge the legitimate place of uncertainty. By achieving balance, we avoid the prospect that either certainty or uncertainty will trample our humanness (Nussbaum, 1986).

This chapter is devoted to achieving a balanced perspective on teaching in school by offering first a story and then a close, critical reading of that story. The story, which concerns an episode of school policy making by teachers, bears closely on teaching itself. My first purpose in criticizing it is to point out elusive elements of teaching that dwell covertly within it, which teachers as well as policy makers on all levels need to recognize. It is also to acknowledge openly and to embrace the messiness of the democratic school.

But I have another purpose, too. The story is a consulting story, constructed bit by bit over the course of more than three years. It was an effective consulting story in terms of its capacity to reflect the concerns of its audience, the teachers who figure in it and who read and discussed its various drafts. I think it is also a conventionally good case study.[2] Its narrative and what might be construed as its findings conform reasonably well to the canons, such as they are, of case study research.[3] It is well grounded in that much documentary evidence supports it; the perceptions of key participants and even marginal participants jibe with it; and it resonates well with theories of how schools work. It reads like much case study research on school policy, having the same structure, texture, and plausibility. Nevertheless, and here I reveal my other purpose in telling it, it lacks a textual liveliness sufficient to the task of portraying the great uncertainties at the heart of it, and it is too self-confident. Careful methodology in the production of such stories—at least in the social-scientific sense—is not enough to do justice to the complexity of the lives they touch. Textual liveliness and the cultivation of critical reading are also very important.

The first of these, textual liveliness, is a synthesis of subsidiary values: presence of multiple perspectives, complexity of narrative design, richness of imagery and trope, symbolic power. These are aesthetic values, and aesthetic values by and large are not currently cultivated in what continues to be regarded as the social science of educational research. Some critics of this situation, however, argue persuasively that certain areas of educational research are especially in need of heightened aesthetic awareness (Bruner, 1986; Gilligan, Brown, & Rogers, 1988; Eisner, 1991). In my view, case-level research on schooling is one of these areas, requiring textual methods attuned to contingency and uncertainty. As Nussbaum (1986) has shown, rich narration is the classical language of contingency and uncertainty, so my suggestions for change run in this direction.

On the other hand, I understand the problem. We cannot expect even a minuscule proportion of researchers on schooling and teaching to write like Toni Morrison. But we can at least expect researchers who work in these areas to acknowledge the complexity they find there, even if they cannot portray it; and we can expect them to honor this complexity by inviting readers to read critically. An invitation to read critically, though commonly a by-product of aesthetic dimensions (the presence of irony or symbol, for example), may also be issued within the constraints of ordinary research discourse. All that is needed is an old researcher's dance, the two-step—though it is often more honored in textbooks of research methodology than in practice. In this dance the researcher first advances an argument with the understated certainty that inheres in the rhetoric of the case study, the report, the monograph. Then, as gracefully and unapologetically as possible, the researcher steps the other way, by means of systematic doubt, into deliberate and principled uncertainty. One step says, "I think I know something"; the other admits, "but I can't be absolutely sure, because, you know, schools are very complex."

THE STORY: A CRISIS OF INCOMPLETES

Bright High School is a charter member of the Coalition of Essential Schools. The teachers of Bright voted to join the Coalition by more than a two-thirds majority, a vote that came after the teachers' union negotiated a special contract clause forbidding teacher layoffs at Bright for five years. The vote was taken at a historic low point in the school's ethos, marked by an interrelated mix of circumstances: faculty morale slump and frequent administrative turnover, a low attendance rate and a high dropout rate among students, a poor image in the community and a general neglect of the school by the city's central administration, a deterioration of the school's physical plant, and a great waning of teaching and learning energy in classrooms. As one might gather from this list (given also some awareness of how race and schooling intersect in America), Bright is an urban high school, ghettoized, subject to that queer characterization "majority minority."

Following the vote to affiliate with the Coalition, and with the assistance of the Coalition staff, Bright secured a large grant from a philanthropic foundation to support its proposed Bright Essential Program. The grant was used to hire a lead teacher and secretary and also to release four teachers from their regular teaching duties for a semester to plan the program's structure and curriculum. This team was to be the first of a projected four teams, added one at a time over four years in an implementation strategy termed by Bright's principal "the Pac-man approach to high school reform." The teams were planned to function somewhat autonomously in shepherding a cohort of 100 students through all their high school years, though the planning team had some doubts about this part of their plan from the beginning and it was later modified, as we shall see. Part of the grant also went to hire several consultants. A few of these were hired early in order to provide planning ideas, though the ideas they contributed proved marginal in the end. Two others were hired later, as resident consultants, expected to supply ongoing support rather than design expertise.

Among the structural innovations planned by the first team and lead teacher, four were especially important: a schedule providing large blocks of teaching time ("double periods"); the provision of five additional planning periods for teachers per week and the allotment of two of these to team meetings; a grading scheme inspired by mastery learning theory (Bloom, 1976), whereby students may be awarded only the grades of *A, B,* or *I* for incomplete; and an unspoken assumption that policy and curriculum would continue to be formulated democratically, as during the planning semester. These were the most important planned innovations because they cut across the grain of Bright High School regularities. In doing so, they tended to focus and conserve reforming energy, protect against reform slippage, and generate continuing invention. One, however, caused some trouble, too.

In the calm of the planning semester, a grading policy that foreswore *F*'s, *D*'s, and even *C*'s seemed, almost by the mere threat of its presence, quite suited to overturning the school's culture of failure and mediocrity. In its insistence on high standards for everyone, the policy seemed to the planners a logical response to the Coalition call for a single high standard, but combined with a signal to kids used to low standards and failure that the kids were not about to be abandoned by their teachers. Such a signal—again in the calm of the planning semester—was presumed to carry great motivational force. From the start, this grading policy was more than a policy; it was also a symbol of its creators' intentions to strive to achieve that state envisioned in the shibboleth of 1980s high school reform, excellence *and* equity. For some teachers in the program, it became an article of faith, a crystallization of their belief in their power to make a difference.

Its symbolic weight protected the policy from the full force of reality's first assaults. At the end of the program's first grading period, 78% of the students earned an *I* in at least one subject, with 24% earning *I*'s in three or four subjects. At the end of the second period, these figures changed to 71% and 41%, respectively. The teachers kept their policy, but had difficulty struggling simultaneously to collect new work due and old work overdue. Even the two who tried to individualize their curriculum so that students could work at different

paces faced problems, especially the proliferation of preparation demands. Soon other concerns arose for everyone: how to keep track
not only of incomplete assignments but of incomplete quarters and,
eventually, incomplete courses; how to hold together a class divided
among the complete, the partially complete, and the incomplete; and,
especially, how to teach without the teacher's old stick—do this or
fail.

Following the advice of the consultants, two of the teachers managed to gain relief from some of the record-keeping fallout by repack-
aging old assignments into what they called "exhibitions" (borrowing
the term from Coalition parlance). Their colleagues, however, saw
some threat to course integrity in this effort—an implicit message to
the kids: Don't bother with the small assignments because you can
always do the big one at the end. In fact, most of the kids who skipped
the small assignments skipped the big ones, too, and the incompletes
kept piling up throughout the first year. By spring, the grading policy
that permitted them seemed the program's albatross—still symbolic,
but intolerably burdensome. How to manage its weight—or whether
to continue to manage its weight—became a topic of nearly every
planning meeting. Sometimes these meetings were quite stormy,
though the most stormy of them were typically followed by calm
ones, as if in a cycle protecting patience through venting.

Meanwhile, the program's Parents Advisory Council expressed
continuing support for the policy, taking the orthodox view that it
protected standards without writing any kids off. The kids themselves, on the other hand, took a different view. A poll conducted in
the spring by the short-lived Student Leadership Committee reported
greater dissatisfaction with the *A/B/I* grading system than with any
other facet of the program. Voicing this dissatisfaction vociferously at
one school meeting, several students demanded that their teachers
"bring back the *C.*"

At about the same time, the lead teacher became uncomfortable
with the policy. He had been one of its chief promoters during the
planning period, having worked successfully with a similar policy in a
previous school. As sometimes happens, however, what he thought he
was promoting and what some team members thought they were es-
tablishing turned out to be somewhat different. He believed that students should work at their own pace and that no one should progress
to new work until they had completed old work. This was what he
called a "continuous progress model," and he regarded it as the practical heart of the policy. He was dismayed, however, to find that several
of his team colleagues disagreed. They argued that his model would

lead to teaching by worksheet, as kids grew progressively more differentiated from one another. The English teacher especially championed this argument. She had once taught in an exclusively individualized way as a reading teacher and had found it unsatisfying. She wanted to be able to bring the energy and insights of the whole class to bear in discussions of texts. To her, the policy did not necessarily require self-pacing, just the opportunity for kids to make up missed work.

The lead teacher argued hard for changes, but he was unable to achieve a consensus of support for any. Each of his suggestions seemed to threaten the interests of one or more team members. Meanwhile, an anxious feeling arose within the team that consensus itself might be destructive. Wouldn't consensus inevitably involve somebody having to give in? One problem was that the group lacked familiarity with democratic mechanisms, whether of a consensual or majoritarian variety. The chairs of meetings tended to play partisan roles, undercutting discussion. Team members seemed reluctant to state their positions fully or clearly for fear of putting these positions at risk. Several found clear evidence of disagreement distressing rather than the first necessary condition of negotiation. Everyone seemed to want to make his or her own separate peace with the problem, echoing in this small way the retreat behind closed doors that characterized the larger school. For their part, the consultants cautioned against any tampering with the policy. They hoped that the pressure of the mounting incompletes would drive the team to experiment with new structures and new styles of teaching. Thus the first year of the program ended with something of a policy stalemate.

Year two brought a second team to the program, whose members arrived already anxious about the crisis of the incompletes. They were teachers from the larger school, where the policy loomed large and menacing in the program's image. Their anxiety about the policy complemented the dissatisfaction felt by the lead teacher, and the chemistry of this connection broke the stalemate, though it failed to halt the crisis. In a summer meeting between the program's first and second years, the lead teacher proposed two policy changes that were adopted with scant opposition. He considered these merely stopgap measures, as he explained to one of the consultants afterward, but his success in achieving them prepared him to achieve bigger changes later.

First, the students got what some of them had said they wanted: *A/B/I* became *A/B/C/I*. Then some also got what they didn't want, namely a demotion. Students regarded by their teachers as impossibly incomplete (slightly less than one-fifth of the whole group, including some who had passed several quarters of some subjects) were put under the care of the new team and told to start the program all over again. The combination was an inventive stroke from the point of view of managing student reaction: The anger of the ones "left back" was effectively muted by the claim that the program had heeded students' demands.

Nonetheless, the mass demotion contributed to the fact that the new team's kids proved much more difficult to handle than the old team's kids had been. Some were aggressive and even abusive toward one another and toward their teachers, and they didn't do much work. Although the old team's students had included both ninth and tenth graders, the new team's kids were all ninth graders. Some were severely in need of socialization, their teachers claimed, and the demotees played a role in this socialization. Some of this was salutary, no doubt—the demotees were proof, after all, that one can be demoted even under this strange new grading policy. Still, several team-two teachers emphasized another effect. They claimed that some of the newcomers had learned shortly after arrival that they didn't have to do much work, and that unless they didn't do *any* work, there wasn't much their teachers could do to them. The situation was complicated by the fact that the program had managed in its second year to attract an even more heterogeneous group of kids than in its first year. There was not only the group said to be in need of socialization, but also a group of middle-class black students who had been admitted to Latin High School, the public prep school across town, but who hoped to find in the Bright Essential Program an equally challenging academic experience within a predominantly black student body. A further complication for team two was that it felt less in control of the program's curriculum, policy, and ideology than team one, which had invented all three. So team two's teachers were at once less inclined to believe in the efficacy of the grading policy, less aware of its subtleties and ramifications, and less confident of their power to change it if they chose.

Meanwhile, the lead teacher became more determined than ever to achieve major changes in the policy. He launched a long, tortuous bicameral policy-making process aimed at accommodating the competing interests at stake in the crisis. Throughout the winter and early spring, in meeting after meeting of first team one and then team two, as well as occasional joint meetings (but there team two was often silent, as they yielded to the veterans), the lead teacher slowly hammered out a new grading policy. The word-processing document he used to keep track of this painstaking work, printouts of which circulated nearly daily between teams, included a legend of notations beside a string of policy features: This passed by team two but not by one, this tabled by team one and not yet considered by two, this passed by team one but amended by two, and so forth.

Parents, students, and the principal were all apprised of the effort underway, and their input considered at various points, but the real policy making—the messy negotiation of it—remained among the teachers, with consultants close at hand.

The entire process resulted in a new and intricate grading policy, which was passed by a somewhat uneasy consensus of the teachers in the spring of the program's second year. It contained eight carefully worded provisions and imagined several structures to be fashioned—such as a semester system of "half-courses" with an accounting of credits earned each September and January; "make-up" classes wherein students, coached by a "make-up teacher," work on overdue assignments packaged in "exhibitions," created and evaluated by their old "teacher of record"; "repeat" classes wherein kids recycle in some novel fashion through a failed half-course. Yes, *failed*. The new policy brought back the *F,* but it also kept the *I*—to be awarded only on the basis of a contractual arrangement specifying how and when the course may be completed: "Ten days before the end of the half year, students who have not completed their work must apply in writing to their teacher for an Incomplete Grade. This application may or may not be accepted by the teacher." The policy also introduced another old feature in a new guise: "crossover flexibility." Students would continue to be assigned a home team of teachers but, depending on their rate of course completion, would be taught some half-courses by teachers from other teams.

The consultants fretted throughout the long negotiations over whether such provisions as "crossover" and the return of the *F* meant wholesale return to Bright regularities, whether a "make-up" course would be anything more than a study hall, whether a "repeat" course would be anything more than a bottom track for recidivists. In the end, they trusted the teachers' feeling that the program's advising system, high parent involvement, high morale, and good attendance would render these new elements different from their analogues in the larger school. So they, too, joined the consensus behind the new policy—not that it would have mattered otherwise: The teachers were in charge and intended to stay in charge.

Despite apparent consensus, however, nearly everyone associated with the program worried about whether changes of the magnitude envisioned by the policy, including so much shifting of students from class to class each half-year, could possibly happen. Some also worried darkly about whether the lead teacher really wanted them to happen, whether the principal would allow them to happen, and whether the policy might not collapse of its own gigantic weight. Indeed the principal did express concerns privately to the lead teacher and to the consultants, but he stuck resolutely to his commitment to let the program's teachers make their own grading policy.

The new policy was complex, but the real source of anxiety was not the complexity but the sense that the policy was still only paper. Actual policy, the kind one may be unanxious about if not necessarily pleased with, is paper plus experience of the way things play out by and large—experience of the subtleties and soft edges of policy that may not show on paper but that provide flexibility in practice. It is one thing to say that there will be "make-up" classes, even to schedule them. It is another thing to have a sense of what happens in such classes, or of how they function in relation to the courses from which they spring. It is one thing to speak of basing incompletes on contracts. It is another thing to have written many such contracts and to have lived through the fulfillment of some and the breaking of others. These other things, all manifestations of practical knowledge, take time to develop and require experimentation.

Before such experimentation could begin, however, the program had to experience a jolt. The jolt was necessary to shake off some of the powerful regularities inherited from the larger school and district. It is a school and district experienced in swallowing up all but the boldest changes. Administering a sufficient jolt required the right opportunity. The lead teacher found one the following January, about a year after the adoption of the policy. By dint of much effort, laboring long hours over a little Apple computer, he managed to reschedule a critical mass of failed and incomplete kids. The result was that the teachers gained a sense that the policy's bottom line held. Now they could believe enough in its other features to experiment with how these features might play out in practice.

"Why weren't we told?" some parents complained when they found *F*'s on their children's report cards—though they had all been warned. The kids, however, heeding the warnings in time, amassed the highest overall passing rate for any quarter in the history of the program. Team one, facing the prospect of the program's first graduation, managed to encode months of discussion, all the fine points compressed in the policy, into a Bright Essential Program transcript. This turned out to be quite a simple document actually, but one impossible to imagine a year or even several months before. The consultants, having chronicled the story to this point, more or less as you have read it, urged the program now to turn a page, start a new story, this one aimed at the overturn of still deeper regularities.

But this was not yet possible. In fact, the story of the incompletes was not over. Certain of its conflicts eluded resolution for two more years. One of these concerned larger regularities of Bright High School. A single jolt was not nearly enough to kill these. A feature such as quarterly grades accumulating to yearly averages, for example, though presumably superseded by the terms of the program's policy, lived on not only in the expectations of guidance counselors, central office transcript-keepers, parents, and kids, but also in the planning, teaching, and evaluative practices of teachers. A powerful and sometimes unconscious norm was at work: Yes, I give a "final" grade at the end of the first semester, but the first semester is still only the first *half* of Algebra I or Biology. Or, put another way, I can't simply divide American History and pretend that kids who know nothing about what happened before the Civil War can have a fresh start in learning about what happened after. The reversion to habit in such cases typically happened behind a closed classroom door. Of course, nobody's classroom doors were fully closed in this program, given frequent team meetings and common planning time, but neither were they ever fully open. There was, for example, almost no team teaching, and little talk about teaching at planning meetings, which were much more frequently devoted to talk about policy, administrative matters, and the needs and problems of kids. Especially lacking was any talk about how the policy was working out *in practice*. This is somewhat paradoxical since for many teachers in the program, collective decision-making and implementation were the indispensable soul of the program. The solution to the paradox can be found again in the regularities of the larger school and system. There policy is handed down, then variously followed, subverted, or ignored without much consequence. There implementation is always problematic but never talked about. The program's teachers were merely continuing this old habit.

Still, the wish for new regularities was powerful, too. This is why the crisis of the incompletes flared up dramatically again when word leaked out: Teachers were interpreting the policy with great latitude. Suspicions were aroused that the culprit was more than a separate peace this time—perhaps even a conspiracy to subvert. It was rumored that one teacher never gave incompletes. A whole team had given *F*'s rather than *I*'s on progress reports. One consultant told a new teacher that the policy allowed teachers to limit students' opportunities to make up old assignments. This remark proved to be a trigger. One teacher, angered by what she perceived to be the consultant's effort to accommodate policy to practice, argued that accommodation ought to run the other way. Implicit in her argument was an acknowledgment that democratic policy making does not necessarily mean finding a way to please everybody, that lines must sometimes be drawn and individual positions compromised. This teacher wished especially to recall the program to what she regarded as its first principle: to provide students, formerly victimized by low expectations and lost hope, multiple chances to succeed. The incomplete grade was an indispensable tool in this effort, she reasoned. To give *F* rather than *I* on progress reports or interim grades, she argued, was to give a message exactly opposite of what the program ought to give. To tell students that they could not make up important assignments was contrary to the program's goals. Yet some teachers were doing both these things under the guise of "policy flexibility."

Her voice activated others, especially the program's new lead teacher (the old lead teacher having recently been promoted to principal at another city school). The new lead teacher rewrote the policy to emphasize the role of the incomplete and to reduce some ambiguity that several teachers regarded as responsible for the "policy flexibility," and then used the occasion of its consideration by all four teams as an opportunity to demand commitment to carry out policy in a uniform way. After two hours of rather calm discussion, resulting in some additions and deletions to the draft, an amended policy was adopted, though with some opposition still evident. Although the crisis abated considerably that day, opposition still sputtered along for a number of months, often having a demoralizing effect. Then, rather surprisingly, on the last day of school of the program's fourth year, the leader of this opposition and the lead teacher jointly offered still another amendment to the policy. This passed unanimously, and the crisis seemed finally over.

THE STORY, CLOSELY READ

As I claimed in introducing it, the story you have just read, though a useful consulting story, lacks sufficient textual liveliness. Consequently, deep currents of the crisis elude its grasp. This is partly a function of the work the story undertook. If it too neatly wraps up the details of an immensely complex and uncertain situation, this was in the immediate interests of its participants, who needed to get on with other business. In this respect, the story might also serve the interests of students of school policy who need—at least early in their study—digestible stories from practice.

But for other purposes—to serve the longer term, reflective interests of participants, for example; to contribute to research; or to go beyond an introduction to school-policy study—what is wanted now is the next step: a close and untidy critical reading. What follows is an attempt to provide just that. The reading will follow a structure framed by classic narrative questions: Who? Where? When? What? and Why? The answers to these questions will, however, overlap considerably.

Who Are the Kids?

Virtually all we know about the clients of change in this story is that they are "majority minority," somewhat "incomplete," and resistant in various ways to their teachers' good intentions. What would they say—beyond "Bring back the *C*!"—if there were room for them to say anything else in this story?

Several students below talk about their incompletes. Between the lines, they say how it feels to find oneself suddenly "student as worker," to face intellectual demands that one is unaccustomed to facing in school, indeed to face caring attitudes that one is unaccustomed to facing in school:

> I have an incomplete now and it's all my fault but because of all the frustrations, I just said, "Forget it. I'm not doing work for awhile."

> There's so much work . . . and they've never explained much of anything. We're a pretty good class, but we're not perfect. We don't understand all this stuff. . . . I have cousins at Madison High School [another city high school] and they don't do anything like what we're doing—why should I? Personally, I prefer [work]book-work. . . .

> Often I let homework go to the last minute, but with this class the work is so substantial that once I get to the point of doing the work, it appears so insurmountable that I don't do it.

> I'll never catch up. . . . I can't spend five whole hours doing homework. . . . I baby-sit, work, clean house, do laundry. Sometimes I do homework at 5:30 in the morning. I get my mom to wake me up. Can you believe that?

> It's so confusing in this class that you don't know what to do. It's so confusing, you don't know where to start.

I get real angry when I don't understand something so I don't do it.
(quoted in McQuillan, 1988, pp. 18–21)

As the story reads now, its conflict is rather impersonal: between "high standards," "course integrity," "excellence and equity" on the one hand; and, on the other hand, "record-keeping fallout," "wholesale return to Bright regularities," and "the school's culture of failure and mediocrity." Student voices like the ones above complicate the plot by overlaying this conflict with a more personal one: between each teacher's own commitment to make demands upon his or her students, and the students' persuasive and even touching appeals for leniency. One cannot appreciate the tortuous quality of the policy-making process chronicled in this story without understanding that the teachers ceaselessly faced this conflict. Nor can one appreciate the appropriateness of the complex policy that evolved, or the reason why it took so long to evolve, without understanding that the forces that comprise the conflict are irreconcilable. As Elbow (1986, p. 152) puts it, only teachers with the genius of Jesus or Socrates can manage to be in the same instant immensely supportive and also fierce. All other teachers must manage the contrary calls of high standards and sensitivity, justice and kindness, by fending off their exact demands. Typically this is managed by constructing a teaching persona and a classroom community within which pushing and caring find some balance (Lampert, 1985). That is why many school policies are in practice, if seldom on paper, as complex as the final version of the Bright Essential Program's grading policy. They must fit intricate and frequently contrary circumstances, shifting continually among different values.

The addition of student voices might also introduce an irony of considerable importance in illuminating another dilemma of teaching: While students frequently ask for conflicting things, they expect unconflicted responses from their teachers. Every teacher knows explicitly the second part of this paradox, typically having learned it painfully during the first years of teaching. Waller (1932) put it well in his classic study of teaching: "The teacher whom students like and admire above all others is the teacher who knows what it is all about, and boldly demands his rights, all of them, but no more" (p. 225). But Waller also understood that no teacher ever really knows what it is all about. He grasped the whole paradox: that the same students who expect certainty provoke uncertainty, if in no other way than by virtue of the conflicting meanings embedded in who they are, what they need, what they say and do. In his appreciation of this fact, Waller was unlike many who have studied teaching in his own day and in ours, and he was also unlike many teachers themselves, who feel conflicted and regard this feeling as evidence of failure.

In fact, to feel conflicted in teaching is a healthy and authentic response to the conditions of teaching. Recognizing this, a teacher will still act with confidence but will face up to the uncertainty rather than deny it—show a confidence that is something other than a stony mask. Such a teacher will foster believing because believing moves people forward and helps people learn; but the teacher will leave some room for doubting, too, because doubting is crucial to thinking and essential to the teacher's effort to model thinking for students. Obviously, the development of grading policy is a matter for professional judgment and leadership. It should not, for example, be formulated in a town meeting where teachers and students both have voting power. On the other hand, it is a matter requiring a good deal of thought as well as leadership. The grading policy dilemma at Bright High School provided teachers an opportunity to model for their students how difficult issues may be addressed and resolved, how new institutions grow and communities develop. If the teachers had had a clearer sense of the legitimate place of uncertainty in professional judgment, I think they might have permitted their students some structured way of contributing to the grading policy debate. Instead, a research team found them very hesitant to do so. The original lead teacher, for example, though he was in some respects a champion of student voice, expressed his hesitations to the researchers about even involving students in discussions of the crisis of the incompletes. He was concerned that divulging the teachers' questions would leave them open to manipulation (Muncey & McQuillan, 1988). Although he launched major structural initiatives to empower students—the convening of "advisory groups" and of "town meetings"—the powers of these forums remained ambiguous and the roles played in them by teachers and students ill defined. One student complained, "When we have these meetings, nothing ever gets done. When we suggest something, nothing happens. . . . We've asked for about twenty things and only got one. That's a bad percentage" (quoted in Muncey & McQuillan, 1988, p. 28).

The addition of student voices to this story, particularly in the right juxtaposition, might also illuminate still one other chronic tension in teaching. Consider the following voices, both responding in writing to the identical assignment. The first is represented by a whole text, the second by an excerpt from a much larger text.

Text 1. In the early coloial period the children tended to be treated as little adults and by doing this there parents crushed the children drivce for independence for such fieling might advance the childs drive for independnce. And for this the puritans were a stricked kind of people for exmapal if a kid cursed or hit their parents puritan law specified the death penalty. The women of this time were no more fortunet eather they were toled to hold there tongue until they were told to speak by there husbes or fathers. But the man had all the privlges they wanthed thay were abal to workl were they wanthed go were they wanthed. in short the man had all the power they wanthed.

Text 2. During the course of time we discover that humans do have values and those values whether great or small eventually hurt or help that person. That persons individual values is neither right nor wrong for that person but is his own. They can be changed but seldom ever do to an extreme. In this paper I will explain the values of the Early Colonial Period and how they helped and hurt the people of that period. . . .

Puritan mothers and fathers were taught to enforce discipline rather than affection. Puritans believed that too much love and affection would take the childrens thoughts off God. They were taught as children themselves that after six there was no childhood or puberty. Children were usually dressed as little adults. . . .

These voices were first presented to me as an example of the contrasts in skill levels that Bright Essential Program teachers find among students in the same class. One contrast involves basic conventions of written standard English: Where the second is appropriately dutiful if occasionally neglectful, the first is seriously inattentive. Another contrast involves rhetorical convention: While the second's experimentation with topic sentence and structural cues suggests maturing in progress, the first's fast and unstructured argument may signal a serious though certainly not hopeless stall.

Many teachers, pressed continuously by the need to reduce the impossible complexity of a roomful of unique human beings, and socialized by various tracking schemes, might rush to judgment on the basis of these two contrasts. So, the first is low-level, the second mid-level; the first remedial, the second college-bound; the first is from the lowest stanine, the second from the middle or middle-high, and so forth. Such sorting judgments are often invested with so much belief that the outsider, perhaps a parent, may marvel at the precision of the categories and the skillfulness of the diagnosis. Once a judgment falls, it becomes hard for anyone to see, for example, that the first voice above may be more powerful thematically than the second; or that both are trying to say something thoughtful and worth saying, something that happens to bear on the matter of sorting them, since sorting schemes often infantilize at least some of the students sorted.

The Bright Essential Program's philosophy rejects tracking, but philosophy alone cannot mute the call of deeply learned categories or solve the problem of coping with heterogeneity. Considering these voices as paper texts only, I can easily imagine ways in which their authors might productively work together, provide each other insight, help each other grow. In this frame of mind, I am certain not only that this can be done, but that it must. The research community and the community that fosters the adoption of research by practice (teachers' organizations, curriculum organizations, teacher education, and regional educational laboratories) join me in my certainty. On the other hand, were I to meet these voices attached to real kids with real class backgrounds and expectations and fears and school histories, thrust at me suddenly from among at least a dozen other voices, with five minutes perhaps before the end of the "double period," my certainty would melt away. This is not to say that my philosophy would melt away, nor my command of methods for implementing it, nor my sense that I must implement it. It is simply to say that real voices complicate my path.

Nor is the uncertainty they introduce ever simply a matter of what they say, but also of the context in which I hear it and of how I interpret it. As for context, the complication introduced into the crisis of the incompletes by voices like the two above is enhanced by a history of institutional racism. One of the grievances that sparked the Bright High School "riot" of the late 1960s was the racial composition of the school's tracks, whites dominating the top, blacks the bottom. Although the text above that is more likely to be pegged top-track (the second) was authored by a black student, while the other was authored by a white, this fact heightens rather than dispels the historical context. If the racial polarization in the tracks of the old Bright High School were to be reversed in some new set of tracks, that would seem to some a great success, while it would seem to others just one more in the city's long string of failures to achieve real desegregation. In either case, the context adds uncertainty.

More about this last point when we consider closely *where* the story takes place. For now, however, there are *who* questions remaining.

Who Are the Teachers?

For one thing, the story does not even tell us their names. One consequence is that we do not always know their gender either—except, for example, in the case of the first lead teacher, who is male. What difference does it make to know that the second lead teacher is female? Or that two of the three males of the original planning team left the program before the conclusion of the story to take traditional administrative positions elsewhere? The answer is that these details must make a difference, not only because gender always makes a difference in human affairs, but because it is particularly salient in schools for historical and structural reasons. Not only is the first lead teacher of this story male, but also the original two consultants, the principal, both assistant principals, and all guidance counselors and central office administrators involved. A story about the working out of an alternative power structure, which is one way to characterize this story, must obviously take such factors into account. The political norms against which the story's struggle occurs were shaped by what has been called the feminization of teaching in the nineteenth century and by the not-coincidental rise of patriarchal attitudes toward the nature of teaching, the role of hierarchical authority in policy making, and the place of definitiveness in policy itself (Apple, 1988).

Consider the following passage from the story through a feminist lens:

> The lead teacher argued hard for changes, but he was unable to achieve a consensus of support for any. Each of his suggestions seemed to threaten the interests of one or more team members. Meanwhile a feeling arose within the team that consensus itself might be destructive. Wouldn't consensus inevitably involve somebody having to give in? . . . Several [team members] found clear evidence of disagreement distressing rather than the first necessary condition of negotiation. Everyone seemed to want to make each his or her own separate peace with the problem, echoing in this small way the retreat behind closed doors that characterized the larger school. For their part, the consultants cautioned against any tampering with the policy. They hoped that the pres-

sure of the mounting incompletes would drive the team to experiment with new structures and new styles of teaching. Thus the first year of the program ended with something of a policy stalemate.

There is first the matter of certain gender-laden expressions: The lead teacher argues hard; the consultants hope that mounting incompletes will drive the team. These may be merely the arbitrary constructions of a male narrator, yet they resonate with something more subtle in the story. We are told that the lead teacher is at first unsuccessful in his attempts to achieve consensus, that his colleagues (half of whom are women at this point, more later) resist. Their interests seem threatened; they seem unclear as to whether consensus is what they want. They seem to want instead what the narrator calls "separate peace"—an inferior option within the story's construction. But DuBois (1983) offers some insight into possible faults in this construction:

> Traditional science reacts to and builds a consensual construction of reality; that construction of reality is seen as a given, real, graspable. It is to be known from the outside, objectively, neutrally, impersonally. Feminism withdraws consent from the patriarchal construction of reality (p. 112). . . . Scientific method is *not* exclusively or even primarily the method of the erector set or the method of taking things apart and putting them back together in order to understand them. Our scientific methods, as women, as feminists, require seeing things *as they are:* whole, entire, complex. (p. 111, emphasis in original)

Suppose the "consensus" that the teachers at first suspect is this neutral, impersonal, erected one. Suppose their apparent retreats into "separate peace" are instead calculated efforts to achieve a different kind of consensus, one constructed slowly from the inside out, subjective, personal, and complex. Suppose the shaky erected consensus achieved through bicameral legislation functions as a shield for this undercover, alternative consensus building—a shield against the anxieties and meddlesome tendencies of lead teacher, consultants, and even principal (all males). Suppose, while planning meetings are devoted to talk about what to do, classes are already full of doing, a provisional doing that is never fully talked about.

In fact, there is evidence to support such an alternative story. I knew, for example, even when I wrote the original story, that the period of "separate peace," extending roughly from the first signs of policy dissatisfaction through the bicameral episode, was also one of active experimentation. By the middle of the program's second year, according to my count, there were eight distinctly different experiments underway, each testing a provisional solution. I assumed at the time, simply because there was no talk about these different experiments at planning meetings, that they were proceeding in isolation from one another. So the story likens them to the larger school's "retreat behind closed doors." In fact, I now believe that the experiments were connected in an informal network of friendships and other affiliations, supported by lunchtime conversations, evening phone calls, and other informal means. I also believe, however, that the network never became comprehensive, and that this caused trouble.

To explore this thesis, we must enter the story's underground, illuminated by teachers' voices. In this underground, the implicit certainty of a bold policy—its confident attempt to reconcile justice and fairness in grading—rubbed up against teaching's uncertainties. These were embedded in individual teachers' complex systems of belief and doubt, commitment and experience. As with all the certainties that enter actual classrooms—whether found in policies, research findings, or philosophies—the rub caused local adaptation (Lighthall, 1989).

So, for example, one teacher explains that she dared to put at risk an old and definitive balance between justice and fairness, all for the sake of what a new and precarious balance might provide. "I used to be a real rule person," she says. "When the bell rang, you're in your seat, no excuses; you're either on time or you're not. Homework's due the next day or forget it. Some people said my classroom was like a jail, but that I was fair. And I was fair. I was just strict."

Why did she choose to surrender this balance? Perhaps because its definiteness threatened her teaching's liveliness. Even if one believes heartily in one's teaching, it is hard to hear it called jail-like. "When we told the kids they could have some power," she continues, "I really had to learn to ease up. . . . Because of the incomplete system, we accept work any time, not just the day it's due. And because we work in groups so much, I don't mind the chaos."[4] This teacher's experience with the policy was unsettling but transformative, too.

Now here is the voice of a second teacher, also very committed to student-centered teaching and to the principles of the Coalition of Essential Schools. While the first perceives a need to loosen her grip, however, the second perceives a need to tighten hers. To her, the push of the policy feels countervailing. "Other elements of the Essential Program," she argues, "like teacher team support, advisory groups, student conferences, and high standards" make the important difference in fostering student success. By contrast, "the incomplete mark . . . fosters student irresponsibility, lack of work, poor work habits, and student anxiety because of the difficulty of doing work later." She wants some limits set on what she calls "the continuous obliviousness toward due dates," and a shift from use of the indefinite *I* to use of the impermanent *F:* "If Julio saw an *F* earlier, one that could be made up and changed, I believe it would be a sign to him of a need to start working" (personal communication).

One might try to establish which of these two voices has a better objective basis, but I think the effort would be pointless. In fact, they both have a good objective basis within the worlds of their own classrooms, permeated as these worlds are by these teachers' perceptions of their students' needs and of their own. In each case, the teacher's "feel" is the crucial means by which she negotiates a minefield of uncertainties. She cannot ignore it, and her colleagues can expect her to change it only after they have come to terms with its sources, after they have found a way to enter her world in order to make their argument there.

If these two teachers, along with all the others working in the Bright Essential Program, had shared with each other the rationales and findings of their individual experiments, if they had told each other the whole stories of their local adaptations, then the crisis of the incompletes might never have built to its climax, or it might have climaxed sooner. As it happened, however, these teachers were parties to different branches of what I called above the informal network, of which there were a number of branches. So they became policy opponents. On the other hand, they were also the teachers whose jointly proposed amendment on the last day of the program's fourth year ended the formal crisis.

Why did their rapprochement take so long? Why did the earlier informal network remain informal and noncomprehensive? Why, despite the opportunity presented by planning meetings and other democratic forums, did these teachers and other teachers fail to talk to each other enough? I think there are three reasons.

The first is that this kind of talking is hard. Opportunities to do it are not enough by themselves. What is needed also are means by which the talkers may enter each other's systems of value, may consider the peculiar demands of each other's experience and craft. The kind of talk that is wanted touches upon core practice and thus threatens those who prefer to keep their core practice unexamined. The second reason is closely related to the first. Such talk, because it touches realms of deep and chronic uncertainty, cannot be fluent, articulate, and confident. It must be halting, partially incoherent, always provisional in its assertions. The problem is that even in the most avowedly democratic schools and school programs, such qualities of voice are suspect. Certainty is still prized and expected there—not only by administrators, students, and parents, but also by teachers themselves. I think the Bright Essential teachers, though willing to engage in a great deal of uncertain talk about the grading policy in planning meetings and other forums, were by and large unwilling to have their practical experiments with policy discussed there for fear that these experiments might be discovered to be nakedly uncertain.

The final reason the teachers did not talk enough is structural. The Bright Essential Program was, as the story suggests, a pilot project, meant from the start to grow bigger. The point was to build something significantly different from the norm, to build it fast, then to have it devour the norm bit by bit. The story calls this the Pac-man approach to school reform. Indeed, the pilot program was able to go much further and faster in its reform efforts than any schoolwide initiative might have gone. On the other hand, these efforts took all the energy of the program's teachers. They had none left over to prepare their colleagues in the larger school for the devouring phase; nor were there many funds left after the first year for summer or release-time workshops. Meanwhile, the program expanded fast, doubling the first year, growing by a full third the second year and by nearly a fourth the third year, and so on. This growth simply exceeded the capacity of the founding team to initiate newcomers to the policy itself and to its values and practical variants. Moreover, as the program grew, the formal policy changed, but usually in terms that only initiates could comprehend. Furthermore, the program did not expand in a vacuum. Each bite of expansion ate up another piece of physical space in the larger Bright High School. Each bite took another group of kids who might otherwise have attended the larger school and incorporated teachers who used to teach in the larger school. Even though these new teachers were volunteers, they were volunteers with histories, histories that typically involved working in isolation at Bright High School and sometimes involved memories of difficult interactions with the same colleagues who, from another point of view, were now new colleagues.

Who Is the Narrator?

The narrator is, of course, myself—the same self whose perspectives and values deeply affected the teaching described in Chapter 3. Is it not likely that my perspectives and values also deeply affected the consulting described here and—more to the point—the narrating that was a tool of this consulting? Since, as narrator, I hide behind an omniscient voice that even dares to hold the consultants (one of whom is myself again) at an ironic distance, it is difficult for the reader of the story to discern my enormous power in shaping it. When one recalls that the teachers themselves were the story's first readers, then one sees the implications of this difficulty. Is it possible that my construction of the crisis—including even its status as crisis—became the teachers' construction, too, simply by means of the power of my "omniscient" narration? After all, the whole point of omniscient narration is to trick the reader into thinking that what has actually been constructed was instead found (Scholes & Kellogg, 1966).

The question is valuable because it raises the kind of doubt crucial to effective reading, though the best answer to it, I think, does not seriously threaten the story's validity. Of course, my construction of the events surely did have an effect on the collective construction of events, but I believe it just as surely did not determine that construction. Otherwise, one would have to believe that all the other participants' sense of these events—so important to their professional lives—simply counted for nothing against my sense. On the other hand, I believe that my narration may indeed impose too simple a framework on the processes it chronicles—one that may be more a function of the time I had to spend in studying it, and perhaps of my need to feel productive in my consulting, than of the processes' natural dimensions. Although I studied the "crisis" for four years, I believe now that I did not see it through to its end, as the story may suggest. I believe, in fact, that the word *episode* may better suit my story's referent than the word *crisis*—a shift of associative emphasis from the definitive to the periodic. I suspect that fragments of the passions, misunderstandings, and dilemmas I chronicled will surface in other configurations at Bright High School for a number of years to come. That is a thought worth pondering by anyone who hopes to change some other school on a shorter timetable.

Where Does the Story Take Place? And When?

We know from my story that Bright High School is in a city, but we know nothing about the city, and very little of the social forces that it must bring to bear on the school—little, that is, besides the remark that Bright has been "ghettoized." Although the story deliberately does not use what I take to be a pejorative term, *inner city,* the reader may nonetheless be left with the impression that the urban status of Bright and of its students is a kind of prenarrative impairment, rather than a rich and dynamic complex of circumstances actively influencing the events of the story.

In a close and illuminating study of a school policy-making crisis in 1920s Chicago, also involving decision making by teachers, Counts (1928) insists upon attention to setting:

> Amid these smoking, teeming, vibrating, shifting, and kaleidoscopic surroundings, and among these hurrying, pushing, loving, hating, worshipping, playing, and battling groups, the public schools of Chicago live and move and have their being. The theorist might prefer a somewhat more idyllic environment, but the Chicago schools always have been and probably always will be in Chicago. (pp. 27–28)

After detailing the effects on his Chicago story of the mayor and city hall, the teachers' federation and the Federation of Labor, the association of commerce, the press, and the women's club, Counts acknowledges that his complicated picture is still oversimplified, the actual situation being several times more complex.

Most of the factors of setting that Counts considers in his case are factors in the Bright High School case, too, though here again their mere enumeration is insufficient for gauging their impact. One must also understand that this impact is often twisted and intensified by paradox and ambivalence. For example, to be a Bright high school teacher is to be victimized continually by an inbred and distant bureaucracy, to be threatened continually by the political helplessness such bureaucracy tends to induce, and to function within a management-labor relationship conditioned by exchanges of authoritarianism and grievance. On the other hand, it is also to be surrounded by auxiliary help: dropout prevention programs, restructuring initiatives, drug abuse prevention efforts, community service incentives, curricular enrichment projects, and so on. Sometimes at Bright High School meetings, consultants who have been hired to help the school under grants of various kinds outnumber the faculty present.

All the offers of help represent one side of a recent ambivalence among Americans about what to do with their cities—whether to continue discarding them or to resurrect them. Homelessness coexists with conspicuous wealth and power; bustling days give way to silent and dangerous nights. The particular mid-sized city where Bright exists had a median family income of only $16,000 at the time of the story, while the median price of a home was a whopping $132,000. Its department stores and movie theaters are long gone to the suburbs, but its banks remain and its hotels are newly thriving. The mills closed long ago, but high tech is moving in. Although an interstate highway cuts through the city's middle and the bus station recently moved out of town, an architecturally significant train station has just arisen in a gleaming new part of downtown built on land created by a Herculean and very expensive gesture—changing the course of two rivers.

The new acreage is likely to shift the city's center away from the derelict half of the old downtown, which—not coincidentally—is near the poorest residential section of the city where many Bright students live. On the other hand, the move will also shift the city's center closer to the hill where Bright itself sits. Unlike the majority of Bright's students, most of this hill's dwellers are fairly well off. Many are quite affluent. Across the street from Bright High School, for example, is the campus of Hamilton Academy, the most prestigious of the city's several independent secondary schools. Nearby is the posh club, whose members are the city's elite, that shares the name of the high school—the Bright Club.

But once again the contrast is less clear-cut than it may at first seem, rendered ambiguous by the conflict of attitude. Several years ago, the attitude was unconflicted: Bright High School could rot, despite its prestigious surroundings. The cupola on its roof seemed an ironic statement: When the school was built, when it was the high school of the white children of the hill, it had deserved one of the hill's most significant architectural details. Then, having shifted its enrollment from 80% majority to 80% minority, it had come to deserve a cupola of chipping paint and broken windows, a rooftop tank of pigeon excrement. Whenever it rained heavily in those days, the excrement rained down on the interior of the school's library. Today, however, the cupola is gleaming again, the roof completely replaced, and the library refurbished. The bricks that had begun falling off the building's facade have been beautifully restored, along with all the building's masonry; and the fence that had protected kids from falling bricks—and lent the school the look of a medium-security prison—has been taken down. Inside, a quarter of the school's classrooms have been refurbished, and a new workroom for teachers installed. The dingy corridors have been painted in colors more appropriate to the school's name, and the dilapidated lockers that once lined them—with doors twisted from their hinges and frames bent beyond repair—

have all been replaced by new ones. Some local philanthropy and two bond issues, vigorously supported by the mayor and approved by a large majority of the city's voters, paid for all this work.

One may argue that this was merely the self-serving response of a city establishment with its eye on demographic forecasts and the labor needs of high-tech industry, but it nonetheless had real benefits for kids who had never enjoyed such benefits before. Still, it complicates the attitudes and habits of the teachers, bred in the earlier era, the time of pigeon excrement. The complication is not just that there has been a change, that the community may be rethinking its decision to throw away this segment of its children—though this alone requires much adjustment on the part of teachers—but that the word *may* is still the appropriate auxiliary verb, that this rethinking is steeped in ambivalence: an ambivalence that is still expressed, as it often is in America, by a color line.

Ghettoization magnifies teaching's daily doubts, may clog a teacher's work with despair. A Philadelphia teacher, in the opening quote of Maeroff's (1988) book on teacher empowerment, describes the impact:

> You are isolated from everyone. The rest of the culture outside the school doesn't give a damn about you or about the kids you are trying to teach. The school system itself almost regards you in that way. You are in a place where the bells are ringing, but the people who are calling the signals for the schools are in places where they can't even hear the bells. (p. 1)

Such feelings do not determine a teacher's response to work, however, and may even cause one to redouble one's work on behalf of kids whose lives have been dismissed by others. But such feelings can also seem to justify a kind of missionary condescension toward the same kids, or turn into a personal and professional bitterness that victimizes the kids twice over—first robbing them of real teaching, then blaming them for the robbery. Nor are these attitudes—among many other possible emotionally charged attitudes—likely to be found in a pure or permanent state. Every teacher who works in a ghettoized school must cope with the fact that such attitudes come and go and interpenetrate one another in ways often difficult to predict or control. This seems true at Bright for both black and white teachers, though the overwhelming majority of teachers there are white, including all but one of the Essential Program teachers.

What happens when teachers in the ghettoized school find the other side of ambivalence waxing? Clearly the teaching and policy-making energy that the Bright Essential Program teachers bring to their work is proportional to the sense they have—based on financial support, press attention, and lots of visits—that the larger community has begun to care about their effort. Yet their response is still not unconflicted. They, like other Bright veterans, have experienced such stimuli before, and they have experienced withdrawal, too. For example, deep inside the story that many Bright teachers tell of the school's long decline, whose explicit villain is usually desegregation, lurks another villain. To recognize it, one must extrapolate beyond the story's ordinary sequence of events: the voluntary desegregation of the mid-1960s; the disorders, or "riot," at Bright in the late 1960s; and the response to this disorder—structural changes, curriculum changes, the hiring of minority teachers. Still later, in the mid-1970s, an economic bust began. It swept away the youngest teachers, among whom were key proponents of the changes that had been made, and it left others to tell the story. Just as importantly, it wrecked many of the changes themselves, thus trifling with people's commitments and promoting cynicism. One veteran of the riot and post-riot years told me the story one day of why he could not stomach the changes then underway within the Essential Program, though he also admired them. In the early years of the 1970s, he confessed, he had yearned for "better" students than the poorly skilled students then beginning to flood Bright. But one day he took the time to listen to his students, and they said something like the following: "We want to work, Mr. Wright, but we can't read this stuff you give us." So he went out and got a second master's degree in reading, and started a reading program. It lasted until the worst budget crunch, and provided him, he told me, the best years of his career while he was running it, but then left him tired and cynical when it ended.

In a study of the intersection of life cycle and teaching, Huberman (1989) accounts for the special tension between a teacher's need at a given time of life for experimentation or stability or disengagement, and the extraordinary uncertainties of teaching. "The problem," he says, "is that too many contingencies within the school are beyond the control of teachers" (p. 48). Among these contingencies are all the ones recounted in this and earlier chapters, including at least one contingency of setting: that the mayor one day, responding to economic crisis, might order the superintendent to cut out of the budget the very thing that gives you the courage you need to cope with all the other contingencies.

At the moment, the political standing of the Bright Essential Program is solid, despite the early 1990s economic bust. Yet the program's teachers are all victims nonetheless of the legacy of boom and bust in their high school. It weighs on their capacity to make policy in unseen ways: What if the ax falls some day? How changed do I want to be? How much can I afford my core practice to be touched? It may have no effect in the end on what these teachers do or say, or how they vote on a policy issue, or how much or how little they reach out to this or that nearly hopeless kid, or how much they take to heart this or that principle of the Coalition of Essential Schools. Nonetheless it adds more uncertainty to their working lives.

How would some better accounting of social forces, as Counts called the complications of setting, change the story of the crisis of incompletes? First, it is important to note that social forces do not array themselves in ways likely to serve the simplest interests of a story's plot. The complex and shifting feelings that may arise between a Bright teacher and student caught in some crossfire of social forces do not fit the relatively clean narrative thrust of most case-writing. They demand a textual place outside the press of plotting toward a resolution, where in the form of what is called a "trope"—literally, a turn of speech—or compressed into a symbol, they may provoke the reader to stop and wonder.

Perhaps some small piece of the story of teachers struggling toward the resolution of policy tensions might be set in a hallway against the busted, twisted lockers that filled the Bright corridors throughout the crisis. Perhaps in some quick turn of phrase the story might evoke the irony inherent in the impressions these lockers made on so many visitors come to see an urban school reforming from the inside out, a school dedicated to making kids take responsibility for their own learning. Or the story might even manage to evoke a still more complex irony: that the condition of these lockers—actually the consequence of fifty years of wear and neglected maintenance—was often presumed by visitors and new teachers to be the wreckage of the "riot" of twenty years before, and often blamed therefore—by means of a racist association—on the kids who go to Bright today. Such irony, such textual liveliness, might help readers better comprehend students' resistance to "completeness."

What Is This Story About? And Why?

According to the story, a group of teachers, left largely to their own devices to follow the nine principles of the Coalition of Essential Schools, made four important design decisions: (1) to establish a different schedule involving "double periods"; (2) to provide time for teachers to plan together; (3) to commit to an *A/B/I* grading system; and (4) to continue formulating curriculum and policy democratically. The story does not say that the teachers also decided to teach in a different way. This is an especially interesting omission, since Theodore Sizer, Chairman of the Coalition of Essential Schools, frequently distinguishes the Coalition from other high school restructuring efforts by claiming that it is out to shift pedagogy, not just structure (Sizer, 1989). Putting aside for a moment whether the story may distort the teachers' actual commitments by overemphasizing their structural deliberations, we might wonder at how four key commitments reduce to one as the story unfolds. Why does the story focus on grading policy? Why, for example, does it view the program's efforts to develop democratic habits through the lens of this single issue?

Lighthall (1989) advises us to put aside materialist notions of school problems as being either real and worth working on, or imagined and distracting. All school problems are imagined, he suggests, in the sense that they represent a mobilization of *minding,* a collective framing of the otherwise unframed and uncertain stuff of actually lived school life. To have a crisis at all—any crisis in which there is some collective sense of the problem—is perhaps the best and only possible first step of school reform. This is because the pattern of status quo is cemented by what Lighthall calls stable localism, the habit of defining a problem in one's own isolated terms, of lacking the capacity to see it otherwise. This is a state of blocked collectivity, in which reform of any kind is impossible because the necessary parties to it typically lack not only common constructions of reality, but also any awareness of this as a problem. Any crisis is better than none at all in the sense that it awakens people to their differences.

It seems to me now quite unsurprising—though I often regretted it at the time—that the Bright Essential Program would focus its first growth anxieties on a crisis in grading policy. This is because grading policy is one of a small number of common means of definition in the teacher's indefinite world. Among the others, I would list seating plans, definition of lateness and punctuality, specification of talk or silence, determination of course or unit duration, definition of reading levels, determination of curriculum level or track, and definition of the scope and boundaries of subjects. Of course, these are all matters of arbitrary judgment, at least theoretically: whether students sit in rows or a circle, whether two minutes late is late or still on time, what kind of talking is OK and not OK, whether Algebra I lasts for a year or longer, whether Linda is a bluebird or a robin in reading, whether this class is "college-bound" English or some other kind, whether history can include art.

Those who are unfamiliar with the teacher's world, including many who would reform teaching in this way or that, often regard teachers as obvious dolts because they seem to behave as if these were fixed matters rather than arbitrary ones. This is ungenerous as well as unproductive, because it overlooks pressures from outside and inside teaching to erect false little certainties. The teacher who speaks as if being an "honors kid" or a "vocational kid" were a matter fixed by genetic code is, after all, putting into thoughtless schooltalk a social-class distinction expressed by the community in dozens of other ways and often insisted upon as a condition of its support for the school. Similarly, teachers who speak as if the scope of Biology, grade-five Mathematics, or level-4 American History were immutable join thoughtlessly in a conspiracy of false certainty hatched far away from their classrooms—in the offices of textbook specifiers and textbook publishers, in conferences of curriculum specialists, in state and district bureaucracies, in testmakers' factories, and so forth.

I do not defend thoughtlessness. I merely point out real pressures to avoid thoughtfulness. And I situate these pressures within a world plagued by chronic uncertainty, where little certainties, however false and sometimes pernicious, nonetheless gain legitimacy by offering some respite.

To understand more fully the crisis of the incompletes, and why it is about what it is about, it helps to know that the Coalition of Essential Schools has deliberately set out to overturn some of the common artificial fixes in high school teaching. Especially targeted are inflexible course duration ("seat-time" in Coalition parlance), tracking, and tight subject boundaries. By demanding much unfixing, the Coalition burdened the Bright teachers with even more uncertainty than teachers ordinarily endure. The Bright teachers knew from the beginning that this was the price of involvement, and by and large they were willing to pay it. On the other hand, they focused the crisis of unfixing on one thing at a time, grading first.

This is not to say that by focusing on grading they ignored other more important matters, much as it may seem, nor that they displaced energy that might otherwise have gone readily into changing the way they teach. On the contrary, there is evidence to suggest that the focus on grading policy was a means for handling a much broader agenda of change: a collective "minding" of deeper and chronic dilemmas of teaching—whether to push or care, whether to individualize or group, whether to emphasize justice or fairness, whether to stand fast or negotiate. The policy crisis in one area of practice—namely, grading—may also have enabled change in other areas of practice by helping to dissolve false certainties that accrue among these deep dilemmas.

On the other hand, if the teachers in the Bright Essential Program had been less inclined toward the clean definition that a new grading policy seemed to promise, if they had been more mindful and tolerant of the chronic uncertainty of their work, then they might have chosen a less tortuous path. I do not fault them for the inclination. I could hardly do that, since I was, of course, a party to it. I merely mean to call attention to the only remedy for this inclination that I can imagine: to be part of a whole profession that is mindful and tolerant of uncertainty. In the end, I believe that a close reading of the Bright teachers' story points beyond their circumstances—our circumstances—to the professional gap that Perrone (1991) describes well:

> We work in a field that has a very long history. This may be obvious, but that history is not something we think about enough. . . . We need to know that many committed men and women over many hundreds of years have seen in teaching the opportunity to build a safer, more humane, and economically productive world. Their stories, the ways they conceptualized their work, help connect us across time and place, enlarging our understanding of the roots of our work and providing us considerable personal and professional inspiration. (p. 120)

This gap demands yet another kind of reading—to regard uncertainty in teaching from a broader perspective than the one provided by one's own practice, collegial conversation, or school work. This kind of reading is the focus of the next and final chapter.

6

Reading for a Profession

Because it spans generations, a profession can offer its members guidance in how to live with their work over time. In teaching, this ought to mean guidance in dealing over time with the chronically uncertain relations among subject, students, and teacher. When I was a young teacher, I needed visions of relations I could emulate, if not quite match. Later, I needed a push to free myself from convenient treaties in the relations of my teaching. Still later, I needed reassurance that my continuing struggle with these relations had real and positive effects on kids and through them on the world. These are all conditions that by and large cannot be soothed by the scientific discourse of educational research, nor by the bromides that constitute much of the other professional discourse in teaching—by journal-talk and conference-talk and in-service-workshop talk. I think they are conditions that instead demand heroic stories.

This may be an odd idea, but it is not a sentimental one. It is meant to sharpen critical awareness of teaching, not dull it. By "heroic stories," I do not mean Mr. Chips stories. I mean bold and angular stories, instead, rich work histories honestly told by the workers themselves. I mean stories layered thickly enough to lend depth of field to readers' otherwise thin perceptions, stories that offer the critical grip their readers need to read their own teaching. So I mean stories to read on long trolley trips, stories to read and discuss with colleagues, stories to set against our own experience in schools.[1]

Meet, for example, Maggie, Sylvia, and Wig: three heroes of teaching whose lives and work span the twentieth century. They are all teachers who had great adventures and who managed against the odds to write about them (there can be no hero without the heroic tale). In their writing they are two mature women and one mature man, with sixty years of teaching among them and even more served in support of teaching. Thus they are heroes against the grain of popular culture, where the heroic teacher is often a young man, one who left the field early, having saved a handful of kids, having proved the system incorrigible. These three are heroes especially because they stayed on, and because the courage and skillfulness they put into staying illuminate the three chief commitments of professionalism in teaching, the best braces in the struggle to endure the uncertainties of teaching. Maggie reveals the first—to hitch one's purpose in teaching to the achievement of democracy; Sylvia the second—to reflect upon one's self as a teacher; and Wig the third—to hold oneself accountable for the effects of one's teaching.

Maggie Haley, an important figure in the struggle to define the American teacher and the work of American schoolteaching, died in 1939 without having found a publisher for *Battleground: The Autobiography of Margaret A. Haley.* She wrote it originally to strengthen the hand of her Chicago Teachers Federation in a struggle with rival unions. Her strategy in this regard is in the book's construction: to inspire solidarity by portraying the Federation's work—and, implicitly, the daily teaching of its members—as a ceaseless struggle for democratic values against oligarchic interests. In this vision of the teaching life, the teacher believes resolutely in the transformative power of a community of learners; she takes her stance among the uncertainties of the daily work with her eyes turned to a vision of the world as her students might re-create it someday. It is not enough to strive for students' individual improvement, she seems to say, or for some sense of one's own technical competence. One must teach for a democratic future. As it turned out, Haley *wrote* for a democratic future, too: Forty years after her death, Robert L. Reid rescued her story from oblivion, and found a climate finally hospitable to her ideas.

Sylvia Ashton-Warner began her career of experimental teaching among the Maori people of her native New Zealand in 1939, the year Haley died. The great fruit of this career, as Ashton-Warner saw it, was the invention of what she called a "creative teaching scheme" for teaching reading to young children. The scheme took what we call today a whole-language approach, characterized by a focus on children's spontaneous attachments to words and by use of children's own writing as texts for reading. The scheme was undergirded by Ashton-Warner's passionate and somewhat quixotic psychological theory. Children are possessed, she thought, by volcanic forces, the consequence of aggressiveness and sexuality. These forces must vent, she felt, in either destructiveness or creativity. When creativity is chosen, destructiveness dries up. So the teacher in her infant room, searching for children's key words—the words that at a touch may unlock life's organic forces—searches in effect for the keys to world peace. The grandiloquence of the image reflects the passionate tone of Ashton-Warner's teaching and writing, while the image itself reveals the inward focus of her method. The authentic teacher teaches, she suggests, by connecting with her students on a visceral level, which demands of the teacher that she stay closely in touch with herself.

Like Haley, Ashton-Warner had some trouble getting published at first. Finally, in 1958, she encased a more direct account of her teaching in a successful novel, *Spinster,* combining romance with a didactic purpose. Today, one finds this teacher's story and its account of a teaching method still in print, with its fictional envelope removed, in *Teacher,* published first in the United States in 1963. It may be the most intimate and most revealing account of teaching ever published.

In the same year, 1963, a Cornell undergraduate named Eliot Wigginton left pre-med to major in English. He planned to be a writer, but also suggested in a diary entry that year that he might take up teaching as a way to support himself while writing. Actually, his career turned out quite the other way around; in an important sense, the writing supports the teaching. Two years into his first teaching job at an academy in the northern hills of his native Georgia, Wigginton and his students founded a remarkable classroom magazine called *Foxfire,* dedicated to Appalachian folk culture. His students became folklorists and serious writers and editors. The magic of the magazine, now twenty-five years old, has to do with the evidence it provides that kids can make a substantial contribution to their community even as they learn from it. Its success has spawned progeny: more than a dozen books, some of them best sellers; a Tony Award–winning Broadway play; the release of a number of folk music recordings; the preservation of much folklore and numerous artifacts of Appalachian culture, including a handsome collection of log structures; the establishment of a regional press; the launching of a major national effort to reform teaching (Wigginton, 1989; Wigginton & Students, 1991).

The roots of the last of these offshoots stretch back to 1975, when Wigginton privately published a methods book (Wigginton, 1975) addressed to the many teachers throughout the country who had written to ask him how to integrate regular English teaching with the production of a magazine like *Foxfire.* He later revised this book for Doubleday, which published it in 1986 as *Sometimes a Shining Moment: The Foxfire Experience.* In making the revision, he also seems to have made a discovery: that the principal commitment of his teaching life was only incidentally associated with what had made him famous—classroom publishing and the promotion of folk culture. He learned that what he really stood for, and what he wished to promote, was a kind of pedagogy that locks hard onto kids. His own commitment as a teacher arises from intense attention to what his kids think and do and learn. It does not arise from fiery political commitment, as in Haley, who hardly ever mentions kids; nor from passionate introspection, as in Ashton-Warner, for whom kids are more objects of missionary attention than learners. Wigginton's teaching, his writing about teaching, and his teaching about teaching all follow the kids closely. *Sometimes a Shining Moment* documents twenty years of his effort to know kids, push them, and hold himself accountable for what they learn.

Maggie's, Sylvia's, and Wig's writings about teaching all originated as limited practical gestures: to inspire the rank and file, to keep track of an experimental method, to give others methodological guidance. Yet all three acquired a more elaborate purpose as they proceeded, a classically heroic purpose: through a portrayal of self, to illuminate and pass on the moral principles of a career. The effort is more stunning in each case because the career itself seems to span eras. So many details of Maggie's Chicago story seem to leap across the century to the story of today's Chicago schools. Sylvia begins her career in a New Zealand wilderness, fretting about the periodic visits on horseback of itinerant school inspectors, but ends it on the other side of the earth in Aspen, Colorado, the venerated teacher of a new generation of progressive teachers. Wig, unmistakably part of the generation that lionized Sylvia, has nevertheless managed by means of a career in only two schools to recapitulate the entire history of secondary teaching in America—from the age of academies to the shopping-mall high school—sustained by the visions and admonitions of his century-leaping mentor, John Dewey.

In their writing, each of these teachers conceives the moral principles of his or her career as a means by which one may hold a teaching life intact in the face of the immense uncertainties that continually threaten to split it. In the process, Maggie turns our attention to what we teach: Just tune it continually to democratic values, she argues, and the rest will fall into place. Sylvia calls attention to our teaching selves: The courage to keep teaching, she suggests, is best supplied by a capacity to inquire into one's own teaching self, to understand and forgive one's self. Wig remembers the kids: The teacher can know his own effects, he says, and find incentives there to keep going. Thus, starting from one of the three points that I used in Chapter 1 to define the uncertain territory of teaching, each of these teachers outlines a path across it. Together they provide a comprehensive map of professional development in teaching, which is why I say reading them is reading for a profession.

MAGGIE HALEY

Maggie Haley was born in 1861, daughter of an Irish immigrant who once marched his children promptly out of a lecture on phrenology (the skull-reading ancestor of intelligence testing) when the lecturer made a sneering reference to Susan B. Anthony. Maggie's childhood was spent successively on a farm, in a village, and in a small town. At age 19, completing a pattern of migration that, as her editor notes, mirrored the shift of population in her time, she took the train to Chicago. But she did not leave her prairie values behind.

In the big, soon passionately big-shouldered city, she studied the craft of teaching with the famous progressive, Colonel Francis W. Parker of the Cook County Normal School. Maggie's own fiery persona seems foreshadowed in her recollection of Parker:

> He roared, he growled, he stormed, he banged. . . . He shook dry bones in things and in people. He scared the wits out of students, and he terrified teachers. He sent for parents and shamed them into aiding their children. He was Reform Rampant—and I watched him with unterrified glee. Never in all my life have I feared anything or anyone, least of all established authority; and in him I somehow sensed the fundamental justice of his attitude and saw the need of his method. (Haley, 1982, p. 24)

She taught grade school for twenty years, sixteen of them in the same school on the South Side of Chicago. However, she tells us virtually all we learn about this part of her life in a single sentence, part of a paragraph that then characteristically sweeps off into comments on affairs of the larger world. Haley is a hero for her efforts to protect the home of teaching, the classroom, but unlike Ashton-Warner and Wigginton, she did all her heroic work far from home.

After teaching all day on the second day of the twentieth century, Maggie closed her desk at the Hendricks School, with every intention, as she tells it, of opening it the next morning. Instead, she left the schoolroom forever. What stole her from the practice of teaching was the first major "battle" of the fledgling Chicago Teachers Federation (CTF). In January 1900, she became its Business Representative—in practice its lobbyist, ideologist, tactician, chief spur, and firebrand.

She was to remain all these things throughout the next thirty-five years, through all the many battles portrayed in the book she called *Battleground* (Haley, 1982). Like the first one, which was aimed at overturning a taxation system that taxed working people to pay for schools but left some big corporations nearly tax-free, all of her battles and those of the CTF pitted the teaching women of Chicago's grade schools against the forces of privilege.

At least that is how she constructs her life's story—forty years battling in "a war of privilege against people . . . waged in and around the public schools of Chicago" (p. 270). In this construction, she remains a teacher throughout. "I have usually visioned myself as so integrally part of the teaching force," she says in the coda to her autobiography, "that, although I have not been in a schoolroom for almost forty years, I record myself, almost unconsciously, as a teacher" (p. 270). The privilege she battled had many guises—sometimes arraying itself as economic interest, as in the tax battle; sometimes as political interest; sometimes even as progressive reform, as in the effort to introduce modern management into the schools. Haley saw a single figure beneath them all: She called it the "industrial ideal . . . monarchical and military," aimed at the overthrow of democracy (p. 86). She saw it as a teacher, and in a feminist light.

To understand why Maggie Haley's autobiography was lost for more than thirty years and is now worth celebrating, one must see her as a teacher-feminist. She was a suffrage crusader who managed also to train her feminism on an institution close at hand. There she discovered what we in the late years of the century are only beginning to realize: that a feminist light illuminates key problems of schooling in America. To be fair to us, it was perhaps easier to know this in her day, given the blatant assertions of such opponents as William R. Harper, president of the University of Chicago and author of the Harper report. The latter was hailed by Nicholas Murray Butler of Columbia University and the National Education Association (NEA) as the definitive document of modern school management. Harper not only asserted in his report that more male teachers were essential for school modernization but also proposed that, as a recruiting incentive, wage increases already promised to all the grade school teachers of Chicago be awarded only to men. Maggie saw more than the immediate affront. She associated Harper with the benefactor of his university, John D. Rockefeller, and what the latter epitomized in terms of economic exploitation and the concentration of wealth. Similarly, she hated Butler and his NEA not only for their disdain of the largely female teaching force, but also for the effects of that disdain: the exclusion of classroom teachers' voices from so many of the key structural decisions made in these years of massive growth in American public schooling.

Always as much the pragmatist as the radical, however—much like Sylvia and Wig—Maggie stayed in touch with the NEA, being the first woman to speak at one of its annual meetings and the engineer of the election in 1910 of its first woman president, Ella Flagg Young. By various means over many years, she tweaked the noses of the NEA men, who stayed in charge despite Young's tenure and who continued to regard Maggie, in words she attributes to Butler, as a little woman of wiles and witchery. Meanwhile, she was determined to build another kind of teachers' association, at least for her Chicago colleagues—a real labor union. In 1902, she led the CTF in its decision to affiliate with the Chicago Federation of Labor. The CTF, the first body of teachers to affiliate with labor, is a direct antecedent of today's American Federation of Teachers.

The decision to affiliate with labor (Reid calls it an "affiliation of women teachers with hod carriers, teamsters, carpenters, and horseshoers" [Haley, 1982, p. xii]) was as controversial in Haley's day as, for example, an assertion in our day that in certain respects teachers should identify less with *professionals*—doctors and lawyers—and more with *craftspeople*—gardeners, actors, hairdressers. The controversy in both cases arises from the perception that such associations diminish the respectability of teaching. However, Maggie's perception, steeped in prairie progressivism, though destined to seem antique if not suspect in post–World War I America, was that identification with working people brings true respectability.

This identification "downward" (to employ the pejorative metaphor) was a feminist gesture, too. Maggie understood very well that identification in the other direction would involve an imposition of male dominance as well as a loss of working-class solidarity. The "higher" professions of her day—as indeed of ours—were dominated by men and by what might be called men's ideology. The association in the Harper report, referred to above, of *men* with *modernization* (or in our terms, *professionalization*) is not sexist in a merely gratuitous way. Our contemporary feminist theorists have pointed out the gendered tendencies of such "modern" or "professional" values as rationality, hierarchy, detachment, and the pursuit of power and profit, as well as the gendered tendencies of such traditional teacherly values as caring, connectedness, and nurturing (Laird, 1988). The dominant ideology of teaching in Maggie's day—as, again, in ours—regarded these latter values as "soft"—a metaphor meant to mean unpowerful. Good teachers like her have always known, however, that these values are quite powerful, albeit indirectly so—in other words, that the effect of teaching on learning does not proceed directly by some powerful laying on of hands, but circuitously by a powerful creation of classroom community. So it did not seem at all contradictory to Maggie Haley and her CTF that teachers who practiced "soft" pedagogy would also dare to have a powerful say in policy matters. But hear how surprised an Illinois legislator seemed by this idea. According to Haley, he warned her as follows: "When you teachers stayed in your schoolrooms, we men took care of you; but when you go out of your schoolrooms, as you have done, and attack these great, powerful corporations, you must expect that they will hit back" (p. 72).

Maggie's tale and heroism are constituted on the surface by unremitting willingness to battle seemingly indefatigable foes—to the point where the reader wonders how she could possibly have endured it. This provides her book's Sisyphus structure, where endurance alone constitutes heroism. We feel for her what we feel for the teacher who manages to keep teaching well day after day, year after year, growing older while her students stay always young and the conditions of her work always poor.

But her book has a deeper structure, too. Here the string of battles takes a great turning in World War I, one from which her movement could not recover in her lifetime. She had vigorously opposed American participation in World War I, lining up in this regard with the socialist tradition within the labor movement, falling out with Gompers of the AFL and with the fledgling AFT. "All the great liberal measures," she writes in her autobiography, "were swept away by the mighty conflict. Not merely the legislation of liberalism but the spirit of liberalism went down before it" (p. 181). The effects on the schools were devastating in her view:

> The World War had shown the United States to be one vast and fallow field for all propaganda. The sowers of the seed—those agencies of power and prestige who already knew the methods and benefits of propaganda—realized during the war that the public schools of America were ideal engines for their purpose. As a result, the essential character of the public schools has been changed in these years which have followed the war. Institutions designed to be breeding places of free and individual opinion have been converted into proving grounds for experiments designed to aid and abet established privilege. (p. 183)

   The first effects of the turning on Maggie show in the brittle
narration of her penultimate chapter, which reads as if she had found
an antidote to despair in recounting tactical complexities. In the very
last chapter, however, entitled "The Darkling Plain" (perhaps after
that other worried schoolperson, Matthew Arnold), she recovers her
teacher's voice and tries in an address to young teachers to transcend
the political climate of her last years. Here is the textual hero, very like
the teacher who seeks a long-term influence by means of a powerful
and communally shared classroom experience, a kind of narrative
chute across the immediate uncertainties of teaching. Maggie models
for teachers how raising one's voice may similarly bridge political
uncertainties, may make a contribution over time, though it may have
little immediate impact. In fact, this hero who lost nearly all her
battles in her own day held views that are now undergoing rehabilita-
tion. For example, she was against bread-and-butter unionism. She
once fiercely fought a bill before the Illinois legislature that would
have increased teachers' pensions, because it would also have given
control of the pension fund to the Chicago Board of Education. Her
position, as usual, was not only principled but pragmatic; she knew
well that in Chicago the control of pension funds could be mightily
abused by politicians. Of course, bread-and-butter unionism eventually carried the day in teaching, as in other fields, but is in our day under
fire again from within the unions themselves.
   She was also against vocational education, viewing it as a "vi-
cious" tactic of class division, and she was against the new intelligence testing that established itself in her day as the schools' chief
sorting mechanism. Both are again under assault in our time. She was
against the bureaucratization of schools, which in her day was taking
the firm hold that was to last into our part of the century and which
many of us rail against now. She was strongly *for* giving teachers a
voice in the making of policy and curriculum in their schools. Nor
was this last issue for her a matter of power for power's sake. She saw
a connection, as some of our contemporary reformers do, between
the teacher's interest and the child's: "If the teachers are to teach
children of the nation how to think clearly and constructively on
matters of national importance, they must first learn their own lesson" (p. 272). Her position on teacher education was a derivative of
her position on curriculum: "Instead of running like hares to classes
which give them nothing but promotional credits, they [the teachers]
must study intensely and intensively the real problems of our time and
of our country. . . . Then, having learned the lesson, they must teach

it" (p. 272). Her position on another issue also has a contemporary ring: "Teachers—and teachers only—must undertake the task of setting and enforcing by law the standards for admission to this profession and of discharge from it" (p. 274).

Beneath all these positions is Maggie's sense of education as a continual struggle among diverse parties over values and her commitment to struggle for democratic ones. For her, curriculum was never a settled or obvious thing, but the product of someone's definition. She wanted teachers to have that power of definition, because she knew that only teachers could pass on the power to kids. If teachers were to be the mere purveyors of curriculum, she feared that kids would become the mere consumers of what powerful interests dished out—and that would doom democracy. Here is an excerpt from her remarkable 1904 address to the NEA:

> The narrow conception of education which makes the mechanics of reading, writing, and arithmetic, and other subjects, the end and aim of the schools, instead of a means to an end—which mistakes the accidental and incidental for the essential—produces the unthinking, mechanical mind in teacher and pupil, and prevents the public school as an institution, and the public school teachers as a body, from becoming conscious of their relation to society and its problems, and from meeting their responsibilities. (pp. 285–286)

To accept Maggie's prescription for professional development is to orient one's work so as to foster the attainment of a democratic culture. That is a big commitment for the teaching profession—bigger than a commitment to teach basic skills or even "higher-order" skills, much bigger than a commitment to train marketable workers, even in a postindustrial marketplace. It is not, however, a bigger commitment than other professions dare to make—the medical profession's commitment to extend and enhance life, the legal profession's commitment to foster the rule of law and to protect individual rights under the law. Of course, these professions meet their commitments unevenly at best, but that is irrelevant. Teachers will always meet their commitments unevenly, too. The point is to aim high so as to gain a broader perspective in the daily struggle to keep going. Featherstone (1988) has expressed this very well. Teachers, he says, must dare to sit with their students at exactly the point where life is most vulnerable: where certainties yield, where one must assume responsibility to make meaning in the face of all life's vicissitudes. Drawing upon John Dewey, Walt Whitman, and Mark Twain—as he might also have drawn upon Maggie Haley—Featherstone argues that democracy depends ultimately on having enough kids who have sat at that point long enough in the company of caring teachers to have gained a lifelong tolerance for uncertainty.

SYLVIA ASHTON-WARNER

Had they ever met, Maggie might have thought Sylvia a pompous egotist. But Maggie, by the evidence of the pronouncements that pepper her text, was always too quick to judge others, and often unfair. Still, the two would probably not have gotten along, even given greater openness on Maggie's part: a matter of discordant passions—Maggie's puritan ones, Sylvia's Freudian ones. Wig might not have liked Sylvia, either, and did actually tell me once that he found her *Spinster* protagonist insufferably self-indulgent. In fact, as he surmised, this self-indulgence—though I prefer to think of it as self-assertion, or self-exertion—is not just a feature of Sylvia's fiction. It was a major feature of Sylvia herself; she understood what she managed in a lifetime to understand by filtering it through her most intimate sensibilities, by drawing it into herself. It is impossible to imagine, by contrast, that either Maggie or Wig could ever say, as Sylvia says in one charged passage of *Teacher* (Ashton-Warner, 1963):

> When I teach people, I marry them. . . . There is quietly occurring in my infant room a grand espousal. To bring them to do what I want them to do they come near me, I draw them near me, in body and in spirit. They don't know it but I do. They become part of me, like a lover. The approach, little different. The askance observation first, the acceptance next, then the gradual or quick coming, until in the complete procuration, there glows the harmony, the peace. (pp. 178–179)

This passage—pure Sylvia—is in function, as well as trope, the climax of *Teacher.* "Tall words," she admits, "wild words," but crafted to reveal, by means of intimate confession, something painfully and elusively true about teaching—something even Maggie and Wig would acknowledge: Teaching gives life but also foretells death. The peace that succeeds procuration in her metaphor is not simply the quietness of the classroom once the kids have left for the day. It is the quietness of confidence that builds up slowly over the course of a teaching career, year by year, far below the surface of its manic details. It is the product of the gradually amassing evidence that one's working life has after all made a difference. But it is also the awareness that the purchase of this difference has been at the cost of growing old. The author's confession of the passion that sustains her teaching comes just three pages short of the book's end-piece, a sad and lyrical coda called "Remembering." Here is how betrothals must end, she seems to say there, and how new generations succeed. She recalls the autumn after her retirement from teaching, and her return to the infant room on the first day of school, to a room no longer hers—new teacher, new kids, new ways, even a new building—an architecturally significant new building. Where her postwar "pre-fab" classroom had stood, there is now bare ground. Where her "creative teaching scheme" had been, there is now a shelf of imported readers. She cannot even bring herself to speak to the new teacher in the new room. In *Spinster,* she captures the exquisite pain of this, her last opening day of school, and by extension of every other opening day of school everywhere—the sad awareness which always underlies the teacher's fresh plans and welcoming face (Ashton-Warner, 1958):

> Don't they know that winter follows? You see it in the flowers . . .
> this hope; in the way they flaunt themselves. All colour and tossing
> of heads! You would think they could bloom for ever. Yet what can
> they do about the autumn? It's as much as I can do to walk in my
> garden in the evenings, knowing what I do and they don't. (p. 15)

In her own way, she rails against the loss of time and wisdom. In the contrast of two photographs that punctuate "Remembering"— one of the rickety pre-fab, the other of the modern glass-walled school that succeeded it—one can read Sylvia's pained protest against an institution that assesses itself by physical and other measures that have utterly nothing to do with the quality of life at its heart. A glass wall, a new shiny floor, a shelf of new readers—but a classroom full of sunny coldness now, of alien looks and feelings, of hopelessness. Her protest, like Maggie's—though much quieter, more accepting of the fatefulness of the moment—echoes down the years. Like Maggie, Sylvia also provides a textual chute across the vicissitudes of her own teaching era and of ours. While Maggie names a form of professional commitment transcending generations, oriented to democratic values, Sylvia names another form of professional commitment, also transcending generations, a commitment to teaching as an intimate activity conducted among a community that may dwell in any kind of building. The bricks, the glass walls, the fancy materials, the fancy credentials, the fascination with structure and prescription—all of these, suggests Sylvia, distract the teaching profession from what really matters: the cultivation of intimate connection.

Sylvia Ashton-Warner is the poet of reflective practice. One reads her today not so much for her creative teaching scheme—which may seem quaint, however consistent with some contemporary thinking about language instruction—but rather for her modeling of a teacher's self-scrutiny. Her value is less in what she reports finding in this self-scrutiny and more in the example of her daring to undertake it, her demonstration of how to do it. The reports from her delvings are always fresh, frank, provocative, and sometimes deeply disturbing— as the betrothal imagery may be for some readers, for example, and as some violent imagery and some racist references surely are for many. There are disturbing passages in *Teacher* that nevertheless reveal important things about a teaching life. Here is an example (Ashton-Warner, 1963):

> And how are you getting on with the Maoris? I ask a visiting teacher to the school.
>
> Oh, it's the energy that's the trouble. They're always on the go. But once you've got your foot on their neck they're all right.
>
> I understand. . . . I understand. . . .
>
> I do. But I don't talk about it. I don't try to describe to others the force of the energy of our New Race. Indeed, when I speak of it as "force of energy" I'm grossly understating it. It's more like a volcano in continuous eruption. To stand on it with both feet and teach it in quiet orthodoxy would be a matter of murders and madnesses and spiritual deaths, while to teach it without standing on it is an utter impossibility. (pp. 90–91)

Happily, though she says otherwise, Sylvia does "talk about it" here and elsewhere: this tension between a teacher's appreciation of her kids' spontaneity and her wish to quash it. The acknowledgment of its presence in teaching hardly ever sees print today, especially as it is here, unscoured of the teacher's racial bias.

I wish Sylvia had been as sensitive as she was perspicacious, had dared not only to dredge up the racism of her time and place but to deal with it better than she did. Sadly, she never managed to do what Paley (1979) describes doing in *White Teacher*—noticing *and* correcting the effects of racism. On the other hand, she was not one of those teachers who thoughtlessly claim that differences of race, class, and culture never matter in their classrooms. At one point in *Teacher* (1963), for example, she critically examines her reaction to the fact that a boy named Matawhero has struck a boy named Gordon. She notices and deplores the fact that "something racial began to boil in me, deep down, that the brown should strike the white" (p. 120). At another point in *Teacher,* she recounts wearing a Maori necklace around downtown Wellington. The gesture is meant to challenge the racism of white neighbors and quietly assert solidarity with Maori neighbors. Today it seems a pathetic challenge and a condescending gesture, but the value of Ashton-Warner again is more in her modeling of self-scrutiny than in what she finds. In her lyrical text of words and photos, she provides evidence that all self-scrutiny, however blind-sided, is always valuable in teaching. This is because the teacher's self—bundle of wishes, fears, values, prejudice, and much more—is inescapably central to teaching.

When she teaches, the author says through the persona of *Spinster* (1958), she is composed of sixty-odd selves, each the response to a student's touch. "I don't know what I have been saying," she adds, "or what I will say next, or little of what I am saying at the time" (p. 22). This uncertainty of self and of speech lives along a jagged landscape of mood:

> 1 PM: There are times when I can't teach and this is one of them. There are troughs of effort as well as peaks and this is one of them. There's a lot of noise, a lot of coloured chalk, a lot of music, a lot of reading, some singing and laughing, but a trough nevertheless it is for me. (1963, p. 169)

On the peaks, she is ecstatic, and portrays them throughout *Teacher* in words as well as photos—photos of children playing, running, sliding down a hillside and splashing in a stream, reading intently, looking painfully or contemplatively or soulfully at a lens.

> At each of those times I saw the meaning of life and knew that I saw it. . . . Every time I reached those heights I said, "All my life before and my life after is justified by the wonder of this moment." Many of those moments I have forgotten now but I haven't forgotten what I said. And I trust myself. (1963, p. 169)

When in the troughs, though, she is ravaged by delusions of ineptitude: "If *only* I had the confidence of being a good teacher. But I'm not even an appalling teacher. I don't even claim to be a teacher at all. I'm just a nitwit somehow let loose among children" (1963, p. 168).

The despair is a symptom of a long-festering conflict in her life between her attachment to her own ways of teaching and the guilt she feels in shunning institutionally sanctioned ways. As it does for many teachers in our time, too, this conflict had gendered roots. Sylvia was the deeply intuitive infant-school teacher who was nonetheless expected to work rationally. She was the impulsive artist of the pre-fab classroom prone to what her husband called extreme solutions, subject to occasional nervous breakdowns, deeply apprehensive of the school inspectors, those tall men, as she called them, with "soft voices and gray souls" (Ashton-Warner, 1979, p. 330). She was a woman working at a craft whose norms, as she discovered painfully again and again, were set by men. And the pain was magnified by the fact that throughout her schoolteaching career, she was married to her own headmaster, a kind and thoroughly professional headmaster, whom she loved and who loved her. "The people called Keith the Master and me the Teacher," she says at one point in the autobiography she wrote in Aspen ten years after her husband's death and half a world from his grave (Ashton-Warner, 1979, p. 286). From this perspective of time and place, she seems finally to have begun to understand what she could not have imagined while writing *Teacher,* namely, that much of the tension in her teaching—a tension that had creative but also self-destructive consequences, and that sometimes welled up menacingly in her relationships with kids—was rooted in her ambivalent anger about being a powerless wife twice over. She was married to a husband whose career kept her for many years lonely in the wilderness and neglectful of her artistry, and she was married to an institution that systematically marginalized her ways of knowing and working.

Yet in the end, Sylvia Ashton-Warner became New Zealand's most famous educator—more famous than her very successful husband, Keith Henderson, and much more famous than all the tall and gray-souled men. The irony is that she did this by noticing her predicament, which is to say by noticing her*self* teaching—noticing it slowly over the course of many years; and by daring in several books, fiction and nonfiction, to lay out her predicament and herself for inspection—despite all her fear of inspection.

ELIOT WIGGINTON

Eliot Wigginton lives on a mountain in a log home his students helped him build, at the highest point of a mountainside educational colony he created. The Foxfire Center is dotted by nineteenth-century log structures—a grist mill, a blacksmith shop, a chapel—discovered rotting at other sites, moved and painstakingly reassembled here with the help of students. It is staffed by teachers and others whose work with local kids and with colleagues in the national Foxfire Network of teachers emphasizes teaching and learning rooted in the experience of community, organized into projects, and sustained by a devotion to craft and the cultures that define it.

To understand Wig's work, one must juxtapose this mountaintop preserve of what may seem antique educational values with the modern high school where he has spent the bulk of his career. There he has taught five periods a day, performed corridor duties, obeyed the policy directives of his principal, and otherwise conformed to the traditional patterns of teaching high school in America. His is an ingenious professional orientation, tuned at once to these two settings, respectful of the symbolic value each holds for the kids of Rabun County, Georgia—heirs of Appalachian culture on the one hand, and of mainstream contemporary American culture on the other. Against the background of ambivalence this dual inheritance provokes, Wigginton makes his move. An original *Foxfire* student, Becky Coldren Lewis, interviewed for the book that celebrates twenty-five years of *Foxfire* (Wigginton & Students, 1991), describes the moment:

> I remember trying to interview my grandmother about making lye soap and quilts. She was hard to interview, though, because she didn't measure anything. Besides, I used to be embarrassed that I had quilts instead of store-bought blankets. Wig was saying, "Go and interview your grandparents about how to do this," and I would think, "Why would I interview her, put it in a magazine, and send it to California for somebody to know that about me? . . . that I used lye soap and had never slept under a store-bought blanket." (p. 8)

Why, indeed? Wig provides the answer that perhaps Lewis, today a teacher herself, can only now understand: to use this encounter with one's own roots to hone oneself into a skillful, powerful, thinking person. For twenty-five years, despite the possible distraction of his success as a national educational figure, Wig has resolutely taught Rabun County kids, and has pushed them as he pushed Lewis.[2] When he taught at the Rabun Gap–Nacoochee School, the boarding school and turn-of-the-century rural academy where *Foxfire* was born, he used that school's ways—its moral focus and strictures, its tradition of practical rural work—to ratchet up ordinary expectations (Puckett, 1989). When he moved *Foxfire* and his teaching to the modern Rabun County comprehensive high school—with its departments and electives and its State Basic Skills Test objectives—he did the same thing there. Although his own practice exemplifies a style of teaching worlds apart from that of ordinary high school classrooms, he has insisted by the example of the ordinary setting in which he has practiced for so long, and by means of the advice he gives other teachers, that the style is unimportant. What matters especially, he says, is the pushing, the search for effects, the attention to the kids.

His book, *Sometimes a Shining Moment* (1986), is 438 pages long: Thirty-one chapters divided into three sub-books. As Wig comes close to admitting himself, it is a work that got out of hand. This is partly because he has much to offer and partly because what he offers does not fit easily within a single genre—any more than his career fits a norm. The book begins as a memoir of the founding of *Foxfire:* how Wig came to teach in the mountains, what he found there, how the magazine was born of an urge to teach better, how it took off, and especially how it fosters a kind of teaching that involves the making and conserving of community. But eventually, one gets the feeling, as in reading Thoreau, that the story here is not about a magazine any more than *Walden* is about a pond. At one point, for example, speaking ostensibly of the magazine, Wig actually characterizes the whole uncertain enterprise of teaching:

> False leads and deadends and mishaps and efforts that seemed to have been wasted at the time were—and continue to be—so much a part of the work with a project like ours that one is forced to make a critical decision early on between two simple options: give it all up as a bad idea or shut up and shove on through. That's it. (1986, p. 134)

And indeed that is it. The magazine is merely one teacher's means of teaching well, which is to say struggling fiercely against the deadends, mishaps, and so forth, in order to make a difference in the lives of particular kids, and through them, to leave a mark on the world. To be a teacher and refuse to strive for such power, Wig claims at one point, is unforgivable.

About halfway through the book, the *Foxfire* narrative yields to other rhetorics. One is hortatory, prominent in the chapter entitled "As Teachers, We Can Make This System Work." Another is expository—sometimes excessively so, as in the long examination of ten "Overarching Truths" about good teaching. Another is descriptive—often inventively so, as in the chapter that begins "For those of you who are interested, let me take one of my courses and dissect it" (p. 327).

Whatever the dominant rhetoric, however, the second part of the book, like the first, is full of stories. Wig's stories about teaching, like all stories, construe experience more neatly than it can have been lived. Many have the sentimental roundness that is the textual residue of the teacher's believing in his work despite the constant evidence that to some extent it always fails. But Wig also regularly punctures his own narrative inflation: The magazine's initial success, he says, was not nearly what he allowed himself to believe at the time; a particular student's success with an assignment was not nearly what it might have been, and so on. The deflation is never complete, of course; otherwise why should one bother to read the stories? But it is enough to mirror the teacher's critical reflection. At the end of an argument about the power of believing in the potential of students whom others have called stupid, Wig adds that he must watch himself carefully whenever he believes in such a student. "Sometimes," he says, "I am so eager to prove . . . that the opposite is true, that I inflate the student's 'progress' unrealistically and allow myself to believe great leaps of improvement are being made when that may not be true" (p. 225).

The two best stories in the book, in my view, offer complementary portraits of a teacher's willingness to look honestly at his students. I think of them as the book's electrodes. One comes early, part of the story of *Foxfire*'s founding; the other comes near the end, deep into the book's effort to move beyond *Foxfire*. The current that connects them is a paradoxical thought about the conduct of a key relation in teaching—the one between a teacher and his kids. Open yourself to let them push you, it tells the teacher, but push them back, even past civility.

The first story is a young teacher's story, though the whole point of its recounting is in the endurance of its discovery. It concerns a "ginseng connection" between Wig and a nameless boy described as one of his ninth-grade, sixth-period "losers." The boy hates school and maybe Wig, too, who has been having some trouble with this class. Wig's efforts to relate better to the boy and to the boy's friends in the class—including a willingness to engage them in arm wrestling—have proved counterproductive. One day, the boy tells Wig that he might as well not bother calling his name in the roll call the next week, since he plans to be off hunting ginseng root or "sang."

"Sang?" Wig responds.

"Man," he answers, "you don't know what sang is? It grows in the woods. You dig it up and sell the roots" (p. 69).

Thus begins a subtle twist of fate, wherein Wig and the boy change places. They agree to meet the next Saturday in the woods.

The boy, a masterful teacher in this small domain, shows Wig only what the top of the ginseng plant looks like, then sends him off by himself to hunt for a match. "When you find one that matches, yell, and I'll come help you. I won't be far." And sure enough, nearly an hour later, when Wig finally does make a painstaking match, the boy comes quickly. "I told you I wouldn't be far," he tells his teacher-turned-student. "I've been watching you. You've been looking good" (p. 71). Then the two hunt on for hours, while the boy tells Wig ginseng stories and instructs him in how to plant, dig, and sell the thing.

Nearly twenty years later, writing his book, Wig suggests what the encounter taught him beyond awareness of ginseng. "He had his areas of knowledge and ignorance," he writes, "and I had mine. . . . And there was absolutely no arrogance about his manner. Just an easy self-confidence and assurance and a resulting gentleness. He was a far better teacher with me than I had been with him" (p. 72). Wig would not forget the lesson: that the core of caring in teaching is a willingness to wield one's honest authority in the other's interest.

The second story is an experienced teacher's admonitory story. It is about the consequences of failing to wield enough caring authority—"an illustration," Wig says, "of what happened to me when I trusted my gut instincts too completely" (p. 390).

In 1979, one of his students, Kim, got an idea for a *Foxfire* article from his father, and Wig recognized the idea right away as perfect *Foxfire*. Kim wanted to write about a local man, Colonel Gray, who had financed an effort during the Depression to build a road to the top of Black Rock Mountain. Gray's intention had been to provide work to men who sorely needed it, including Kim's father, and to create a park for the community at the mountain's magnificent but inaccessible peak. Though Gray's first effort failed, the road was finally completed years later by the state and the park built on land that Gray and others donated. But by then Gray's contribution had been forgotten, and he lay in an unmarked grave.

In recounting Kim's experience researching and writing his article, Wig enumerates the signs of a successful learning experience. For one thing, the article was the longest thing that Kim had ever written, and a product of redrafting, which Kim had previously little tolerance for.

[Moreover] the magazine that featured the article was an instant hit. . . . Kim himself received a welcome dose of self-confidence and praise; Kim and his father entered into a somewhat different kind of

relationship from that they had been used to . . . and Kim stepped
beyond himself to help correct what many in the county perceived
as a wrong . . . [learning] something, too, from Colonel Gray's un-
selfish desire to make a contribution in time of need. (pp. 393–394)

Such evidence of their teaching's impact would satisfy most teachers. Indeed, it is solely by the grace of such evidence, when they can
get it, that many fine teachers keep teaching. But for Wig it is not
enough. He deflates his own narrative again, his own believing. First,
he reprints Kim's article, then assesses it coldly—absent the warmth
of all his contextual knowledge as a teacher, absent any excuses. The
writing, he says, is

flat and unemotional and without passion. Each paragraph of the
narration has equal weight; there is no figurative language or color or
sense of pace or momentum. . . . In addition, though Kim learned
about one event that happened during the Great Depression, he
learned virtually nothing about the causes of that depression or its
impact on all of Rabun County or the Appalachian region as a whole,
or the role of government in bringing it to an end. In addition,
because Kim worked largely alone, the rest of the class, which could
have made some real contributions to the work by helping Kim find
other informants (or by adding supplementary interviews themselves
to round out the story as a class activity), was not involved. (p. 394)

This is a bold and rare move—to step aside from contextual
knowledge and apply a cold standard. It takes courage, because holding kids to high standards usually means confronting their premature
satisfaction with themselves. All endorsements of high standards not-
withstanding, there are few teachers or parents or policy makers who
would be willing to tell Kim the whole truth. The move takes courage,
too, because the student's shortcomings reflect the teacher's. Wig
understands this and asserts, in fact, that the point of his story is not to
evaluate Kim, who is, after all, now beyond his reach, but rather, by
means of an evaluation of Kim's work, to criticize himself. Imagine
what Kim might have accomplished, Wig says, if I had only pushed
him further. The experience was a gold mine, he concludes, but he—
Wig—left half the gold in the ground.

My favorite image of teaching's uncertainty—one befitting the
hero—is of a two-headed monster whose mouths bombard the teacher
continuously with one question each. "What is to be learned?" asks
one mouth. "What has been learned?" asks the other. It seems to me
that one way to evaluate teachers is by noticing who fears this monster

or, on the other hand, who thinks it has been tamed or is only an imaginary monster. The latter think, for example, that one can easily make a list of what to cover in a high school English course, or that one can easily define the precise component skills of good writing or of aesthetic sensibility. Ignoring the real ferocity of the monster, they even pretend that such lists can be regarded as fairly stable and that they can be generated completely outside the context of a particular community of teachers and learners—by the Georgia Department of Education, for example. And, of course, they also pretend that the other monstrous question—What has been learned?—can easily be answered by externally devised tests in combination with the teacher's gut instincts.

Wig's teaching and writing warns us that the monster is real and, moreover, that it is a single monster with two heads, not two monsters. The latter insight is important, and particularly difficult to face up to, since a single two-headed monster is harder to fight than two less complex monsters taken each in turn. In other words, it is much easier to plan good teaching, wrestling with all the design uncertainties that this entails, and then, only later, to worry about how to assess its effects. It is much harder to worry about these things simultaneously, much more perilous to one's own sense of competence to remember always that beautiful teaching that does not teach is not teaching at all, and that clever assessment that does not assess what is really important is not clever after all. In the following brief passage, Wig explains how an honest willingness to take on one of these monstrous questions—What is to be learned? What has been learned?—must become necessarily entangled with the other, even at the expense of mucking up the common images of teaching and learning as clean, rational processes:

> A teacher brings someone in from the community to be interviewed and assumes that activity addresses the objective of helping to develop student listening skills. But did it? Really? Probably not. Certainly not by itself, in isolation and without some active teacher intervention before and after—and I mean intervention by a teacher who has finally fought through all the muck and come to an understanding of what that objective is truly and why it's there in the first place. (p. 389)

"Finally fought through all the muck": a good image of teaching as an uncertain craft. Typical Wig, too—whose book carries an epigraph from Aunt Addie Norton:

I tell you one thing, if you learn it by yourself, if you have to get down and dig for it, it never leaves you. It stays there as long as you live because you had to dig it out of the mud before you learned what it was.

AN UNCERTAIN PROFESSION

There is no question, where the craft of teaching is concerned, that "you must learn it by yourself," digging it out of uncertainty thick as mud. Nevertheless, Haley, Ashton-Warner, Wigginton, and many other teacher-writers from our century and other centuries have ensured that you need not learn it *all* by yourself. Contrary to what is sometimes said about it, teaching has a recorded history that can be consulted by those who wish to learn from it. They must, however, be prepared to ferret it out of the stories. An eighty-six-year-old grandmother, Mrs. Queen R. Stone of Milwaukee, once wrote a letter to Wigginton in appreciation of the honor *Foxfire* gives to a kind of knowledge quite like teachers' knowledge of their craft. "Some of my friends, my contemporaries for the most part, seem to regard such knowledge to be something to be hidden and lived down," she wrote. "I'm sure I'm thought to be a little 'tetched in the head,' but the young folks beg for the stories. They seem to have an unconscious need for some reassurance in this uncertain time" (Wigginton, 1986, p. 150).

The young folks may beg for Mrs. Stone's stories, because the stories transcend the uncertainty of rural life without disrespecting it. This is what teachers' stories often do as well for teaching. They engage the relations of teaching with great forthrightness, but admit the fragility of the effort. They implicitly suggest the high probability that in any given week of teaching the teacher will experience what I experienced one afternoon long ago. At the precise height of what I took to be my brilliant peroration on the Trojan War, all my students— every single one—dashed simultaneously to the windows of our classroom to see a great thunderstorm suddenly roar up the hill. Teachers' stories can coach us quietly through such thunderstorms, help us not to lose heart; and they can also ensure over time that our experience of sudden thunderstorms in teaching enriches that teaching. Now I might know enough to run to the windows myself—and hail Zeus. That's the wisdom of an uncertain craft.

Lately, we have grown used to the pursuit of a spurious professionalism in teaching—full of pose and technique, bereft of thunder-storms—but the genuine thing has been available all along. To secure it, we need only have the courage to do what the last four chapters have described: Reflect on our practice, converse with our peers, look critically at the circumstances of our work, and, finally, attend to the voices of experience.

Notes

Chapter 1

1. An important exception is recent research by Lee Shulman (1986, 1987a, 1987b).

2. A notable exception in current research is the work of Eleanor Duckworth (1987, 1991), who closely attends to the complexities of children's and others' efforts to grasp particular ideas. She follows a research tradition that owes much to David Hawkins (1973, 1974). Magdalene Lampert (1985, 1991), whose research focuses more on teaching than does Duckworth's, nevertheless grounds much of her inquiry in close examinations of children learning mathematics.

3. Cochran-Smith and Lytle (1990) point out that the dustjacket of the *Handbook of Research on Teaching* (Wittrock, 1986) describes the contents as "the definitive guide to what we know about teachers, teaching, and the learning process," though the massive volume includes no writing by teachers, nor, by Cochran-Smith and Lytle's count, a single citation of teacher writing.

4. Some documentary basis in special education is essential for due process, genuine parental involvement, state monitoring, and sensible planning. My problem with the IEP as the documentary basis is that it tends to overspecify goals and objectives and is consequently reductive. E. McDonald (1989) has described this problem from the point of view of a special education teacher: "Let's say for the sake of argument that you could figure out a way to demonstrate that Lisa uses periods with 90% accuracy. In the unlikely event that you will ever be asked to prove it, wouldn't it be better to play it safe and go with 75%?" On other problems with IEPs, see Singer and Butler (1987). For a broader critique of the law, see Gartner and Lipsky (1987).

Chapter 2

1. I am by no means the first to propose this. See especially Lightfoot (1983b), Eisner (1976, 1985, 1991), Featherstone (1989), Kagan (1989), and Barone (1990).

2. Eisner (1991), his colleagues, and students practice "educational criticism," which treats observed teaching as a key ingredient—along with material drawn from interviews and other sources—for rich textual renderings.

3. Nussbaum (1986) eloquently undertakes an exploration, by means of classical texts, of how one may be passionately central and intentional though not in control, and of why this balance *must* be struck: "Aristotle reminds us that we, like archers, will be more likely to hit our target if we try to get a clearer view of it. But Aristotle warns against pressing such a view too far: for he shows that each of the strategies used to make practical wisdom *more* scientific and *more* in control than this leads to a distinct impoverishment of the world of practice. . . . Indeed, a creature who deliberated with all the superiority of an acute scientific intelligence but did not allow himself or herself to respond to his surroundings through the passions would both miss a lot that is relevant for practice and be inhumanly cut off from much of the value of our lives" (p. 310).

Chapter 3

1. Just as I am not the first to propose the value of reading teaching, I am not the first to ground theorizing about teaching in a reading of my own teaching. Lampert (1985) does it boldly and well in an essay that was intertextually implicated, as you will see, in my own learning to read teaching. Other imaginative examples include Cazden (1988) and Coles (1989).

2. I do not mean to suggest a duality between a teaching self and a single authentic self, but merely a constructed difference between personal presence in teaching and personal presence in other social situations.

3. I refer again to Nussbaum (1986) (note 3, Chapter 2). "The *Antigone,*" she writes, "has articulated the idea that the right sort of relationship to have with the contingent particulars of the world is one in which ambition is combined with wonder and openness" (p. 310).

4. Johnston (1989) argues that the kind of supervision I describe is probably the only workable kind. In the process, he quotes Robert Stake, summarizing twenty-five years of experience in educational evaluation: "We did not come to be great admirers of American teachers, or their capacity for self-correction, but as with Churchill's view of democracy, it beats the alternatives" (p. 517).

Chapter 4

1. The Study of the American High School was a project of the National Association of Secondary School Principals and the Commission on Educational Issues of the National Association of Independent Schools. It produced three books: Sizer (1984), Powell, Farrar, and Cohen (1985), and Hampel (1986).

2. I began my habit of tape-recording the meetings of the Secondary

Study Group as a feature of this experiment in sharing deliberately constructed anecdotes. We anticipated that the anecdotes would be worth saving, as indeed I believe they proved to be. With the permission and encouragement of the group, I continued my recording habit long after the experiment with the anecdotes ended. In all, I recorded 27 meetings between 1985 and 1990. The quotations from the group's conversations that follow here are all taken from transcripts of these recordings, lightly edited to facilitate reading.

Chapter 5

1. Patrick McQuillan, a graduate student of anthropology who studied Bright and my role there, reminds me that no "native" ever called me a consultant. I think both they and I recognized the value of declining to assign me any formal, unambiguous title. I was just Joe; I was just helping out in this way or that. In fact, as we all knew, I was an insider-outsider, a limbo-spanner, an uncertainty broker. If the term *consultant* seems inappropriate, I think that is because we are used to a kind of consulting that dispenses false certainty. See J. P. McDonald (1989a).

2. In fact, the story is both a consulting story and a case study—a dual purpose evident in its history. The first draft, written during the Bright Essential Program's first year, was presented by Bright High School teachers themselves at a workshop in professional decision making held at Wheelock College, Boston, March 1987. The purpose was to give workshop participants a close view of democratic policy making, and also to solicit their advice. Other drafts of the story were presented by me in various consulting workshops at Bright High School, and also at successive annual meetings of the American Educational Research Association (J. P. McDonald, 1988, 1989b).

3. See, for example, Stake (1988). There is also what I would call a positivist tradition within case-study research, which applies stricter methodological standards than my story can meet. See, for example, Miles and Huberman (1984) and Yin (1984). In my view, this stricter tradition, though valuable as a device of inquiry, loses power as the complexity of its subject increases. In the study of schooling especially, I would complement social scientific rigor with aesthetic ways of knowing—as I argue in this chapter. In this regard, see also Eisner and Peshkin (1990) and Eisner (1991).

4. The quotations here and in the paragraph above are taken from a publication of the teachers' union, unacknowledged in order to protect the teacher's privacy, used with the teacher's consent.

Chapter 6

1. This chapter is indebted to my fellow participants in a symposium on the role of teachers' stories in research on teaching, presented at the annual meeting of the American Educational Research Association in Boston, April 1990. Joseph and Helen Featherstone contrasted teacher storytellers of the

1960s and the 1980s. Marue Walizer (1990) presented a paper on the narratives of Vivian Paley and Sylvia Ashton-Warner. Her paper, "Teachers' Stories as Research and Reflection," inspired me to reread Ashton-Warner and to write about her here. My paper (an early draft of this chapter) was about Margaret Haley and Eliot Wigginton, and Wigginton was himself the symposium's thoughtful discussant.

2. Twenty-five years, Wigginton writes in the introduction to *Foxfire: 25 Years* (Wigginton & Students, 1991), "is just about a career . . . enough time, for example, if you stay in the same community, for your earlier students to present you with a new senior class largely made up of their children" (p. ix). Near the end of the introduction, Wigginton announces that he will take a leave of absence from Rabun County, beginning in September 1991, in order "to help create a new method of training teachers [at the University of Georgia, Athens] in conjunction with several demonstration schools" (p. xiii). Wigginton will continue to teach daily in at least one of these schools. Still, an era has passed.

References

Adler, M. (1982). *Paideia proposal: An educational manifesto.* New York: Macmillan.

Apple, M. W. (1988). *Teachers and texts: A political economy of class and gender relations in education.* New York: Routledge.

Archambault, R. D. (1964). Introduction. In R. D. Archambault (Ed.), *John Dewey on education* (pp. xiii–xxx). Chicago: University of Chicago.

Ashton-Warner, S. (1958). *Spinster.* New York: Simon & Schuster.

Ashton-Warner, S. (1963). *Teacher.* New York: Simon & Schuster.

Ashton-Warner, S. (1979). *I passed this way.* New York: Knopf.

Barone, T. E. (1990). Using the narrative text as an occasion for conspiracy. In E. W. Eisner & A. Peshkin (Eds.), *Qualitative inquiry in education: The continuing debate* (pp. 305–326). New York: Teachers College Press.

Belenky, M., Clinchy, B., Goldberger, N., & Tarule, J. (1986). *Women's ways of knowing: The development of self, voice, and mind.* New York: Basic Books.

Berke, R. L. (1990, February 3). Bennett asserts drug education isn't key. *The New York Times,* p. 1.

Berlak, A., & Berlak, H. (1981). *Dilemmas of schooling: Teaching and social change.* New York: Methuen.

Bloom, B. S. (1976). *Human characteristics and social learning.* New York: McGraw-Hill.

Boyer, E. (1983). *High school: A report on secondary education in America.* New York: Harper & Row.

Bruner, J. S. (1986). *Actual minds, possible worlds.* Cambridge, MA: Harvard University Press.

Buchmann, M. (1984). The use of research knowledge in teacher education and teaching. *American Journal of Education, 92,* 421–439.

Carnegie Forum on Education and the Economy. (1986). *A nation prepared: Teachers for the 21st century.* New York: Carnegie Corporation.

Cazden, C. B. (1988). *Classroom discourse: The language of teaching and learning.* Portsmouth, NH: Heinemann.

Cochran-Smith, M., & Lytle, S. L. (1990). Research on teaching and teacher research: The issues that divide. *Educational Researcher, 19* (2), 2–11.

Cohen, M. (1983, March 2). The public schools can't be reformed from the top down: A "front-line" view of the *Paideia Proposal's* shortcomings. *Education Week,* p. 24.

Coles, R. (1989). *The call of stories: Teaching and the moral imagination.* Boston: Houghton Mifflin.

Counts, G. S. (1928). *School and society in Chicago.* New York: Harcourt Brace Jovanovich.

Cuban, L. (1990). Reforming again, again, and again. *Educational Researcher, 19,* 3–13.

Dewey, J. (1929). *The quest for certainty: A study of the relation of knowledge and action.* New York: Minton, Balch.

DuBois, B. (1983). Passionate scholarship: Notes on values, knowing, and method in feminist social science. In G. Bowles & R. D. Klein (Eds.), *Theories of women's studies* (pp. 105–116). Boston: Routledge and Kegan Paul.

Duckworth, E. (1987). *"The having of wonderful ideas" and other essays on teaching and learning.* New York: Teachers College Press.

Duckworth, E. (1991). Twenty-four, forty-two, and I love you: Keeping it complex. *Harvard Educational Review, 61,* 1–24.

Dweck, C. (1987, April). *Children's theories of intelligence: Implications for motivation and learning.* Address to the annual meeting of the American Educational Research Association, Washington, DC.

Eisner, E. W. (1976). Educational connoisseurship and criticism: Their forms and functions in educational evaluation. *Journal of Aesthetic Education, 10* (3–4), 135–150.

Eisner, E. W. (1985). *The educational imagination: On the design and evaluation of school programs* (2nd ed.). New York: Macmillan.

Eisner, E. W. (1991). *The enlightened eye: Qualitative inquiry and the enhancement of educational practice.* New York: Macmillan.

Eisner, E. W., & Peshkin, A. (Eds.). (1990). *Qualitative inquiry in education.* New York: Teachers College Press.

Elbow, P. (1986). *Embracing contraries: Explorations in learning and teaching.* New York: Oxford University Press.

Evans, P. M. (1984). A dialogue among teachers. *Harvard Educational Review, 54,* 364–371.

Featherstone, J. (1988). A note on liberal learning. *National Center for Research on Teacher Education Colloquy, 2* (1), 1–8.

Featherstone, J. (1989). To make the spirit whole. *Harvard Educational Review, 59,* 367–378.

Foucault, M. (1980). *Power/knowledge: Selected interviews & other writings, 1972–1977* (C. Gordon, Ed.). New York: Pantheon.

Freire, P. (1970). *Pedagogy of the oppressed.* New York: Continuum.

Gartner, A., & Lipsky, D. K. (1987). Beyond special education: Toward a quality system for all students. *Harvard Educational Review, 57,* 367–395.

Gilligan, C., Brown, L. M., & Rogers, A. G. (1988). *Psyche embedded: A place for body, relationships, and culture in personality theory* (Monograph No. 4). Cambridge, MA: Harvard University, Laboratory of Human Development.

Goldman, M. (1990). *Provoking the conversation* [Video]. Providence, RI: Coalition of Essential Schools, Brown University.

Haley, M. A. (1982). *Battleground: The autobiography of Margaret A. Haley* (R. L. Reid, Ed.). Urbana: University of Illinois Press.

Hall, G. E., & Hord, S. M. (1987). *Change in schools: Facilitating the process.* Albany: State University of New York Press.

Hampel, R. L. (1986). *Last little citadel.* Boston: Houghton Mifflin.

Hawking, S. W. (1988). *A brief history of time.* New York: Bantam.

Hawkins, D. (1973). What it means to teach. *Teachers College Record, 75,* 7–16.

Hawkins, D. (1974). *The informed vision: Essays on learning and human nature.* New York: Dyathon.

Herndon, J. (1985). *Notes of a schoolteacher.* New York: Simon & Schuster.

Horton, M., with Kohl, J., & Kohl, H. (1990). *The long haul: An autobiography.* New York: Doubleday.

Houston, H. M. (1988). Restructuring secondary schools. In A. Lieberman (Ed.), *Building a Professional Culture in Schools* (pp. 109–128). New York: Teachers College Press.

Huberman, M. (1989). The professional life cycle of teachers. *Teachers College Record, 91,* 31–57.

Jackson, P. W. (1968). *Life in classrooms.* New York: Holt, Rinehart & Winston.

Jackson, P. W. (1986). *The practice of teaching.* New York: Teachers College Press.

Johnston, P. (1989). Constructive evaluation and the improvement of teaching. *Teachers College Record, 90,* 509–528.

Kagan, D. M. (1989). The heuristic value of regarding classroom instruction as an aesthetic medium. *Educational Researcher, 18* (6), 11–18.

Kidder, T. (1989). *Among schoolchildren.* Boston: Houghton Mifflin.

Laird, S. (1988). Reforming "woman's true profession": A case for "feminist pedagogy" in teacher education? *Harvard Educational Review, 58,* 449–463.

Lampert, M. (1985). How do teachers manage to teach? Perspectives on problems in practice. *Harvard Educational Review, 55,* 178–194.

Lampert, M. (1991, April). *Representing practice: Learning and teaching about teaching and learning.* Paper presented at the annual meeting of the American Educational Research Association, Chicago.

Lightfoot, S. L. (1983a). The lives of teachers. In L. S. Shulman & G. Sykes (Eds.), *Handbook of teaching & policy* (pp. 241–260). New York: Longman.

Lightfoot, S. L. (1983b). *The good high school: Portraits of character and culture.* New York: Basic Books.

Lighthall, F. F. (with S. D. Allan). (1989). *Local realities, local adaptations.* New York: Falmer.

Little, J. W. (1982). Norms of collegiality & experimentation: Work place conditions of school success. *American Educational Research Journal, 19,* 325–340.

Lortie, D. C. (1975). *School teacher: A sociological study.* Chicago: University of Chicago Press.

Maeroff, G. I. (1988). *The empowerment of teachers: Overcoming the crisis of confidence.* New York: Teachers College Press.

McDonald, E. (1989). *Sorry, Anthony, that's not in your IEP.* Unpublished manuscript. Harvard Graduate School of Education, Cambridge, MA.

McDonald, J. P. (1988, April). *Beyond collaboration: The role of crisis and textmaking in a school-university partnership.* Paper presented at the annual meeting of the American Educational Research Association, New Orleans.

McDonald, J. P. (1989a). When outsiders try to change schools from the inside. *Phi Delta Kappan, 71,* 206–212.

McDonald, J. P. (1989b, March). *Story and voice in school policy and research.* Paper presented at the annual meeting of the American Educational Research Association, San Francisco.

McIntosh, P. (1990, October). *Teachers as gardeners.* Address to the Rhode Island Councils of Teachers of English and Social Studies, Warwick, RI.

McQuillan, P. (1988). *Differential constructions of reality: Students and teachers in negotiation.* Unpublished manuscript, Brown University, Providence, RI.

Metzger, M. T., & Fox, C. (1986). Two teachers of letters. *Harvard Educational Review, 56,* 349–354.

Miles, M. B., & Huberman, A. M. (1984). *Qualitative data analysis: A sourcebook of new methods.* Beverly Hills: Sage.

Muncey, D., & McQuillan, P. (1988, February). *Student response to educational reform: Empowerment and the negotiation of change.* Paper presented at the Ethnography in Education Research Forum, University of Pennsylvania, Philadelphia.

National Commission on Excellence in Education. (1983). *A nation at risk: The imperative for educational reform.* Washington, DC: U.S. Government Printing Office.

Noddings, N. (1984). *Caring: A feminine approach to ethics and moral education.* Berkeley: University of California Press.

Noddings, N. (1986). Fidelity in teaching, teacher education, and research for teaching. *Harvard Educational Review, 56,* 496–510.

Nussbaum, M. C. (1986). *The fragility of goodness: Luck and ethics in Greek tragedy and philosophy.* New York: Cambridge University Press.

Paley, V. G. (1979). *White teacher.* Cambridge, MA: Harvard University Press.

Paley, V. G. (1981). *Wally's stories.* Cambridge, MA: Harvard University Press.

Paley, V. G. (1988). *Bad guys don't have birthdays: Fantasy play at four.* Chicago: University of Chicago Press.

Perrone, V. A. (1991). *A letter to teachers.* San Francisco: Jossey-Bass.

Powell, A. G., Farrar, E., & Cohen, D. K. (1985). *The shopping mall high school: Winners and losers in the educational marketplace.* Boston: Houghton Mifflin.

Puckett, J. L. (1989). *Foxfire reconsidered: A twenty-year experiment in progressive education.* Urbana: University of Illinois Press.

Sarason, S. B. (1971). *The culture of the school and the problem of change.* Boston: Allyn & Bacon.

Sato, M. (1989, July). *Research on teaching and in-service education: An experiment to empower wisdom of teachers.* Paper presented at the US/Japan Teacher Education Study Consortium, Honolulu.

Scheffler, I. (1984). On the education of policymakers. *Harvard Educational Review, 54,* 152–165.

Schneier, L. (1990). *Why not just say it?* Unpublished manuscript. Harvard Graduate School of Education, Cambridge, MA.

Scholes, R. S. (1985). *Textual power.* New Haven, CT: Yale University Press.

Scholes, R., & Kellogg, R. (1966). *The nature of narrative.* New York: Oxford University Press.

Schön, D. A. (1983). *The reflective practitioner: How professionals think in action.* New York: Basic Books.

Schön, D. A. (1987). *Educating the reflective practitioner.* San Francisco: Jossey-Bass.

Schor, N. (1987). *Reading in detail: Aesthetics and the feminine.* New York: Methuen.

Sedlak, M. W., Wheeler, C. W., Pullin, D. C., & Cusick, P. A. (1986). *Selling students short: Classroom bargains and academic reform in the American high school.* New York: Teachers College Press.

Shulman, L. S. (1986). Those who understand: Knowledge growth in teaching. *Educational Researcher, 15* (2), 4–14.

Shulman, L. S. (1987a). Assessment for teaching: An initiative for the profession. *Phi Delta Kappan, 69,* 38–44.

Shulman, L. S. (1987b). Knowledge and teaching: Foundations of the new reform. *Harvard Educational Review, 57,* 1–22.

Singer, J. D., & Butler, J. A. (1987). The Education for All Handicapped Children Act: Schools as agents of social reform. *Harvard Educational Review, 57,* 125–152.

Sizer, T. R. (1984). *Horace's compromise: The dilemma of the American high school.* Boston: Houghton Mifflin.

Sizer, T. R. (1989). Diverse practice, shared ideas: The essential school. In H. J. Walberg & J. J. Lane (Eds.), *Organizing for learning: Toward the 21st century* (pp. 1–8). Reston, VA: National Association of Secondary School Principals.

Spacks, P. (1982). In praise of gossip. *Hudson Review, 35,* 19–38.

Stake, R. (1988). Case study methods in educational research: Seeking sweet water. In R. M. Jaeger (Ed.), *Complementary methods for research in education* (pp. 253–265). Washington, DC: American Educational Research Association.

Symposium on the year of the reports: Responses from the educational community (1984). *Harvard Educational Review, 54,* 1–31.

Thomas, D. W. (1985). The torpedo's touch. *Harvard Educational Review, 55,* 220–222.

Walizer, M. (1990, April). *Teachers' stories as research and reflection.* Paper presented at the annual meeting of the American Educational Research Association, Boston.

Waller, W. (1932). *The sociology of teaching.* New York: Russell & Russell.

Wehmiller, P. L. (1985, October). *The miracle of bread dough rising.* Address to the Friends Council on Education Seminar for Teachers New to Quakerism and to Quaker Schools, Philadelphia.

Wigginton, E. (1975). *Moments: The Foxfire experience.* Washington, DC: IDEAS, Inc.

Wigginton, E. (1986). *Sometimes a shining moment: The Foxfire experience.* Garden City, NY: Doubleday.

Wigginton, E. (1989). Foxfire grows up. *Harvard Educational Review, 59,* 24–49.

Wigginton, E., & Students. (Eds.). (1991). *Foxfire: 25 years.* New York: Doubleday.

Wise, A. (1979). *Legislated learning: The bureaucratization of the American classroom.* Berkeley: University of California Press.

Wittrock, M. C. (Ed.). (1986). *Handbook of research on teaching* (3rd ed.). New York: Macmillan.

Wolf, D., Bixby, J., Glenn, J., III, & Gardner, H. (1991). To use their minds well: Investigating new forms of student assessment. In G. Grant (Ed.), *Review of research in education* (pp. 31–74). Washington, DC: American Educational Research Association.

Yin, R. K. (1984). *Case study research, design and methods.* Beverly Hills: Sage.

Index

Absent-mindedness, 27–28, 33
Acting. *See also* Dramatizations
 to arouse students' interest, 33, 35
 relationship between teaching and, 35–36
Acting out, 50
Adler, Mortimer, 44
Advisory groups, 84
Affection, toughness and, 51
American Educational Research Association, 127*n*
American Federation of Labor (AFL), 108
American Federation of Teachers (AFT), 107–108
Anthony, Susan B., 105
Antigone (Sophocles), 18, 126*n*
Anti-Semitism, 62
Apartness, 11
Apple, M. W., 87
A priori assumptions, 3
Archambault, R. D., 60
Aristotle, 126*n*
Arnold, Matthew, 109
Ashton-Warner, Sylvia, 17, 35, 101–105, 107, 111–115, 122, 128*n*
 commitment of, 104, 112
 conflicts of, 114–115
 creative teaching scheme of, 102–103, 112–113
 racism and, 113–114
 on self as teacher, 102–104, 111–115
Autobiographical writing assignments, 25–27

Barone, T. E., 125*n*
Battleground: The Autobiography of Margaret A. Haley (Haley), 102, 105

Belenky, M., 13
Belief and believing
 doubting vs., 18
 power of, 26
 teachers in fostering of, 84
Bennett, William J., 4
Berke, R. L., 4
Berlak, A., 29
Berlak, H., 29
Binary valuation systems, spuriousness of, 21
Blind students, visual dimension of teaching and, 23
Bloom, B. S., 74
Bolter, Henry, 42
Boyer, E., 44–45
Brave New World (Huxley), 64
Brown, L. M., 72
Bruner, J. S., 72
Buchmann, M., 15
Bureaucracies, 93, 109
Butler, J. A., 5, 125*n*
Butler, Nicholas Murray, 106

Capote, Truman, 25–27
Caring, control and, 29
Carnegie Forum on Education and the Economy, 68
Case study research, 72–73, 127*n*
Cazden, C. B., 126*n*
Certainty, conspiracy of. *See* Conspiracy of certainty
Chicago, Ill.
 Haley's career in, 105–109
 school policy-making crisis in, 93
Chicago, University of, 106
Chicago Board of Education, 109

Chicago Federation of Labor, 107
Chicago Teachers Federation (CTF), 102, 105, 107–108
"Christmas Memory, A" (Capote), 25
Churchill, Winston, 126*n*
Classroom discussions
  control of, 36–37, 46–49, 64
  dramatizations vs., 59–61
  gossip and, 57
  and ideology of effective teaching, 59–60
  resolving conflicts and, 46–49
Classrooms
  atmospheres of, 29–30
  constructing meaning of experiences in, 17
Clinchy, B., 13
Coalition of Essential Schools, 73–75, 97–100
  grading policy reform and, 74–75, 89–90, 99–100
  principles of, 69–70, 89–90, 97–98
Cochran-Smith, M., 125*n*
Cohen, D. K., 38, 126*n*
Cohen, Marshall, 44
Coles, R., 126*n*
Collegiality
  avoidance of, 21
  encouragement of, 8
  prevalence of, 10
  in Secondary Study Group, 43
  between tutors and classroom teachers, 40–41
Columbia University, 106
Communities, 94–95
  in rethinking value of ghettoized schools, 95
  socioeconomic portraits of, 94
Computers, teaching with, 66
Conferences, one-legged, 71
Conflict resolution, Secondary Study Group on, 46–49
Consensus building, 88
Conspiracy of certainty, 2–8
  overturning of, 6–8
  teachers in, 5–6, 8
Consultants, 68–100, 127*n*
  genders of, 87
  grading policy reform and, 75–76, 78–81, 87–88, 92

modeling responsibilities of, 68–69
number of faculty members hired compared with, 93
overvaluation of, 68
and policy studies on structures of schools, 68–72, 74–76, 78–81, 87–88, 92
as readers of stories, 71
storytelling by, 70–71
Contextual pedagogical knowledge, 49–50
Continuous progress models, 75–76
Control
  of behavior, 63–64
  caring and, 29
  of classroom discussions, 36–37, 46–49, 64
  on fieldtrips, 53
  for students, 52
Cook County Normal School, 105
Cornell University, 103
Counts, G. S., 93, 97
Critical reading
  to heighten perplexity, 63
  meaning of, 56
  preparation for, 66–67
  by Secondary Study Group, 56–67
  on structure of schooling, 71–72
  of Thomas's text, 56–61
Critical reflection and thinking, 18, 118
Crossover flexibility, 78
Cuban, L., 6
Culture of the School and the Problem of Change, The (Sarason), 42
Curriculum
  democratic formulation of, 98
  grading policy reform and, 74–75, 77
  Haley on, 109–110
Cusick, P. A., 38

Deep-set knowledge, 41
Defensible teaching, 59
Demotions, 76–77
Desegregation, 71, 96
Dewey, John, 2–3, 7, 41, 60, 104, 110
Diagnostic-prescriptive teaching, 5
Discourse. *See also* Classroom discussions
  gossip vs., 57–58
DNA, arousing students' interest in, 33, 36

Doubleday, 103
Double periods, scheduling of, 98
Doubts and doubting
  about lessons, 26
  in reading teaching, 18–19
  teachers in leaving room for, 84
Dramatizations. *See also* Acting
  classroom discussions vs., 59–61
Drug and alcohol abuse, 4, 50
DuBois, B., 88
Duckworth, Eleanor, 14, 125*n*
Dweck, C., 21

Economics, 15
Educational Collaborative for Greater
    Boston, 42
Educational criticism, 126*n*
Education for All Handicapped Children
    Act (P.L. 94–142), 4–5, 125*n*
Education Week, 44
Edwards, Jonathan, 56, 58–60
Effective teaching, ideology of. *See*
    Ideology of effective teaching
Ego. *See* Self in teaching
Eisner, E. W., 72, 125*n*–127*n*
Elbow, P., 18, 53, 71, 83
Enabling, providing vs., 51
Energy, 34–36
Evans, Paula M., 42, 44–45
Experimentation
  encouragement of, 8
  school structure reform and, 89–90

Fairness, balancing justice and, 89
Farrar, E., 38, 126*n*
Featherstone, Helen, 127*n*–128*n*
Featherstone, Joseph, 110–111, 125*n*,
    127*n*–128*n*
Feminism, 88
  of Haley, 106–107
  and professionalization of teaching, 107
Fidelity, 51
Fieldtrips, losing control of children on,
    53
Forgiveness, insistence and, 29
Foucault, M., 16
Fox, C., 58
Foxfire, 103, 116–119, 122
Foxfire: 25 Years (Wigginton & students),
    116, 128*n*

Foxfire Center, 115–116
Foxfire Network, 116
Freire, P., 43

Gartner, A., 125*n*
Georgia, University of, 128*n*
Georgia Department of Education, 121
Ghettoized schools, 93, 95–96
Gilligan, C., 72
Goldberger, N., 13
Goldman, M., 17
Gompers, Samuel, 108
Gossip, discourse vs., 57–58
Grading
  demotions and, 76–77
  reforming policy on, 74–84, 86–90, 92,
    97–100
  of Velcro essays, 26–27
Gray, Colonel, 119–120
Great Depression, 119–120
Gripping in reading teaching, 17–18
Gun ownership, discussions on, 36

Haley, Margaret A., 17, 101–112, 122,
    128*n*
  background of, 105
  commitment of, 104, 112
  feminism of, 106–107
  pacifism of, 108
  on teaching in achievement of
    democracy, 102, 104–105, 110–
    112
Hall, G. E., 71
Hampel, R. L., 126*n*
Handbook of Research on Teaching
    (Wittrock), 125*n*
Harper, William R., 106
Harper report, 106–107
Harvard Educational Review, 44, 56
Hawking, S. W., 7
Hawkins, David, 125*n*
Heisenberg, Werner, 7, 41
Henderson, Keith, 115
Herndon, James, 2
Hesse, Hermann, 31
Heterogeneity, coping with, 86
High School (Boyer), 44
Hinduism, lessons on, 31–32
Hord, S. M., 71
Horton, Miles, 14

Hostility, tenderness and, 21–22
Houston, H. M., 69
"How Do Teachers Manage to Teach?
  Perspectives on Problems in
  Practice" (Lampert), 28–29
Huberman, A. M., 127*n*
Huberman, M., 96
Huxley, Aldous, 64

Ideology of effective teaching, 59–63
  connection between teaching and its
    effects in, 60
  contingency and volatility denied by,
    39
  and good kid/bad kid distinction, 62–
    63
  and good teacher/bad teacher distinc-
    tion, 62–63
  interactiveness in, 60
  pervasiveness of, 62
  preparedness in, 66
  on provision of knowledge, 60
  purposefulness in, 59–60
  torpification and, 60–61
Individualized educational plans (IEPs),
  P.L. 94–142 on, 5, 125*n*
Inner city schools, 93
Insistence, forgiveness and, 29
Instrumental pedagogical knowledge, 49–
  50
Intelligence testing, Haley on, 109

Jackson, P. W., 12, 64
Jesus Christ, 83
Johnston, P., 126*n*
Journal writing. *See also* Reading teaching
  and current rereading, 20–41, 126*n*
  for students, 54–55
  textmaking and, 17
Justice, balancing fairness and, 89

Kafka, Franz, 34–36
Kagan, D. M., 125*n*
Kellogg, R., 92
Kennedy, Edward M., 4
Kidder, T., 7, 17
Knowledge
  base for teaching in, 54
  deep-set, 41
  ideology of effective teaching on
    provision of, 60

pedagogical, 49–50
teachers' commitment to subtleties and
  standards of, 53

Laird, S., 107
Lampert, Magdalene, 28–29, 34, 83,
  125*n*–126*n*
Learning
  mastery theory of, 74
  of mathematics, 125*n*
  role of conflict in, 23
  teachers' willingness in, 66
Lessons and lesson plans. *See also*
  Classroom discussions
  doubts about, 26
  on Hinduism, 31–32
  and observations, 37, 39
  on space travel, 66
Lewis, Becky Coldren, 116
Libraries, doing research in, 40
Lightfoot, S. L., 125*n*
Lighthall, F. F., 70, 89, 98
Linkage, 1–2
Lipsky, D. K., 125*n*
Little, J. W., 12
Localism, stable, 98
Lortie, D. C., 12
Lytle, S. L., 125*n*

McDonald, E., 125*n*
McDonald, Joseph P., 127*n*
McIntosh, P., 23
McQuillan, Patrick, 83–84, 127*n*
Maeroff, G. I., 95
Make-up classes, 78–79
Maori people, Ashton-Warner's work
  with, 102, 113–114
Massachusetts Department of Education,
  42
Mastery learning theory, 74
Mathematics, learning of, 125*n*
Meno (Plato), 57
Merchant of Venice, The (Shakespeare),
  61–62, 65–66
Metamodels of teaching, 65
Metamorphosis, The (Kafka), 34–36
Methods
  codes for, 16
  failures in, 25–26
  idea that teaching is about, 6
Metzger, Margaret T., 24, 58

Miles, M. B., 127*n*
Mimetic teaching, transformative teaching
    vs., 64
Mobilization of minding, 98
Morrison, Toni, 72
Muncey, D., 84

National Association of Independent
    Schools, Commission on Educational
    Issues of, 126*n*
National Association of Secondary School
    Principals, 126*n*
National Commission on Excellence in
    Education, 68
National Education Association (NEA),
    106–107, 110
National Endowment for the Humanities,
    42
National security, schools as risk to, 10
Nation at Risk, A (National Commission
    on Excellence in Education), 68
Nation Prepared, A (Carnegie Forum),
    68
Newton, Isaac, 7
New York Times, 4
Noddings, N., 29, 51
Norton, Addie, 121–122
Nussbaum, M. C., 46, 71–72, 126*n*

Objectives, failures in, 25–26
Observations, 37–39, 126*n*
    direct, 16, 126*n*
    ideology of, 39
    ironies raised by, 38–39
One-legged conferences, 71
Othello (Shakespeare), 64

Paideia Proposal (Adler), 44
Paley, Vivian G., 17, 35, 113, 128*n*
Parents
    certainty prized and expected by, 91
    in school structure reform, 75, 78–80
    teachers criticized by, 31–32
    on writing assignments, 55
Parker, Francis W., 105
Pedagogical knowledge, contextual vs.
    instrumental, 49–50
Perrone, V. A., 100
Personae. *See* Self in teaching
Peshkin, A., 127*n*
Philosophy, 15

Physics, uncertainty in, 7
Plato, 46, 57
Policy flexibility, 81
Policy makers. *See also* Schools, policy
    studies on structures of
    in conspiracy of certainty, 4–5
Powell, A. G., 38, 126*n*
Practical invention, serendipity of, 8
Practice of teaching
    perspectives from, 9–14, 126*n*
    reading teaching and. *See* Reading
        teaching
    reflection in. *See* Reflective practice
    spotting uncertainty in, 11
    stepping outside of, 9–11
    theoretical perspectives on, 15–19
Principals
    genders of, 87
    grading policy reform and, 78–79, 87
    school structure reform and, 73, 78–79,
        87
    teachers observed by, 37–39
Providing, enabling vs., 51
Psychology, 15
Puckett, J. L., 116
Pullin, D. C., 38

Rabun Gap-Nacoochee School, 116
Racism
    Ashton-Warner and, 113–114
    tracking and, 86
Reading
    Ashton-Warner's creative teaching
        scheme for, 102–103, 112–113
    critical. *See* Critical reading
    integrating writing assignments and, 52
    as interpretive activity, 51
    storytelling and differences between
        writing and, 71
    to students, 25–26
Reading teaching, 17–21. *See also* Journal
    writing
    demands made by, 14
    difficulties in, 12
    disclaimers on, 19
    doubting in, 18–19
    elements of, 17–19
    gist of, 11
    gripping in, 17–18
    noticing quirky details and puzzling
        over them in, 56

Reading teaching (*continued*)
  relationship between overcoming si-
    lence of teaching and, 13–14
  and relations of teachers, 13–14
  in Secondary Study Group, 12
  self-revelations resulting from, 28
  textmaking in, 17
  as two-eyed reading, 14
  value of, 21, 41, 126*n*
Reality, building consensual construction
  of, 88
Reductive methods, 3
Reflective practice, 11, 19
  Ashton-Warner as poet of, 113
  avoidance of, 21
  schools for, 13
Reform initiatives. *See also* Schools, poli-
    cy studies on structures of
  failures of, 6–7
Reid, Robert L., 102
Release-time workshops, 91
Repeat classes, 78
Research and researchers
  and case studies, 72–73, 127*n*
  in conspiracy of certainty, 3–4
  in libraries, 40
Research papers, handing in of, 39–40
Ride, Sally, 66
Rockefeller, John D., 106
Rogers, A. G., 72
Romeo and Juliet (Shakespeare), 14

Sarason, S. B., 12, 42
Sato, M., 17
Scheffler, Israel, 10, 14, 41
Schneier, Lisa, 14
Scholes, R. S., 18, 51, 56, 92
Schön, D. A., 11
School reform movement, 68
Schools
  bureaucracies of, 93, 109
  cellular design of, 12, 14
  communities around, 94–95
  desegregation of, 71, 96
  entrepreneurs of improvement of, 2–3
  for reflective teachers, 13
  refurbishing and repairing of, 94–95
  as risk to national security, 10
  suburban teachers in urban, 49
Schools, policy studies on structures of
  active experimentation and, 89–90

case study research and, 72–73, 127*n*
close reading of, 81–100
Coalition of Essential Schools on, 69–
  70, 74–75, 89–90, 99–100
connections and contradictions between teaching as uncertain craft
  and, 67–100
consensus building and, 88
consultants and, 68–72, 74–76, 78–81,
  87–88, 92
critical reading of, 71–72
democratic mechanisms in, 76, 81, 98
demotions and, 76–77
economic conditions and, 96
flexibility in, 81
grading policy and, 74–84, 86–90, 92,
  97–100
and growth of programs, 91
institutional racism and, 86
and managing student reaction, 77
modeling in, 69
narrator in, 92
parents involved in, 75, 78–80
and providing time for teachers to plan
  together, 98
reform planning in, 73–74
and rise of cynicism among teachers,
  96
and scheduling of double periods, 98
setting of, 92–97
storytelling and, 70
students in, 74–80, 82–87, 97–98
teachers in, 72, 87–91
textual liveliness of, 72
timing of, 96–97
on tracking, 86
Schor, N., 46
Scientific method, 88
Seat-time, Coalition of Essential Schools
  in targeting of, 99
Secondary Study Group, 42–67
  on arousing students' interests, 33–34
  background of, 42–43
  on control of classroom discussions,
    46–49
  critical reading by, 56–67
  gossip and discourse in, 57–58
  gripping and, 18
  horror stories heard by, 53
  phases in development of, 43–45
  political aim of, 44

on relationship between teachers and subjects, 33–34
Sizer and, 42, 44
storytelling and, 70
tape-recording meetings of, 58, 126*n*–127*n*
teaching anecdotes read and shared in, 45–56, 127*n*
textmaking and, 17
value of, 12
writings inspired by, 44
Sedlak, M. W., 38
Self in teaching, 20
as absent-minded, 28, 33
alienation of, 49
Ashton-Warner on, 102–104, 111–115
as catalytic and mediational, 24
exuberance of, 23–24
grading policy reform and, 83
self in social situations vs., 126*n*
unreconcilable things reconciled by, 28–29
under wraps, 24
Senate, U.S.
Judiciary Committee of, 4
Labor and Human Resources Committee of, 4
Sex and sexuality, 31, 35–36
Shakespeare, William, 14, 34–36, 61–62, 64–66
Shulman, Lee S., 125*n*
Siddhartha (Hesse), 31
Singer, J. D., 5, 125*n*
"Sinners in the Hands of an Angry God" (Edwards), 56
Sizer, Theodore R., 42, 44, 69, 98, 126*n*
Skills
idea that teaching is about, 6
of students in writing, 85–86
Social classes and milieus
and communities, 94
meanings of, 30–31
teacher-student relationships and, 49
Socialization, school structure reform and, 77
Socrates, 57, 59, 83
Sometimes a Shining Moment: The Fox-fire Experience (Wigginton), 103–104, 117
Sophocles, 18, 126*n*

Sorting schemes, criticisms of, 86
Space travel, lessons on, 66
Spacks, P., 57–58
Special education, P.L. 94–142 on, 5, 125*n*
Spinster (Ashton-Warner), 103, 111–112, 114
Stable localism, 98
Stake, Robert, 126*n*–127*n*
Stone, Queen R., 122
Storytelling
by consultants, 70–71
and differences between writing and reading, 71
by teachers of heroic stature, 101–123
uncertainty transcended by, 122
Students
aggressive learners among, 21–22
appeals for leniency from, 83
applying cold standards to, 120
arousing interests of, 33–36
attractiveness of, 31
certainty demanded by, 83, 91
cliquishness of, 30–31
Coalition of Essential Schools on, 69
compliance of, 39–40
contrasts in skill levels of, 85–86
control for, 52
critical capacities of, 32
demotion of, 76–77
empowerment of, 84, 89
in facing unaccustomed situations, 82–83
genders of, 31
grading of, 26–27, 74–80, 82–84, 86, 97–98
intimidation of, 32
journal writing for, 54–55
passivity among, 21–22
reading to, 25–26
relationship between subjects and, 1–2, 125*n*
relationship between teachers and, 1–2, 13–14, 22, 33–36, 49–50, 54–55, 61, 115, 118–119, 125*n*
resolving conflicts between and with, 46–49
in school structure reform study, 74–80, 82–87, 97–98
social class backgrounds of, 31

Students (*continued*)
  spontaneity of, 113
  teacher observations and, 37–39
  teachers' commitment to nurture and
    support, 53
  teachers evaluated by, 54–55
  teachers' expectations for, 49
  teachers' willingness to be ungentle
    with, 57–61
  uncertainty provoked by, 83
  victimization of, 22
Student teachers, noticing one's own
  practice in eyes of, 11
Study of the American High School, 42,
  126*n*
Subjects
  Coalition of Essential Schools in target-
    ing boundaries of, 99
  codes for, 16
  relationship between students and, 1–
    2, 125*n*
  relationship between teachers and, 1–
    2, 13, 33–36, 61
Suburban teachers, urban schools with,
  49
Suicide, discussions on, 36–37
Summer school, teaching in, 40
Summer workshops, 91
Supervision, limits of, 38–39
"Symposium on the Year of the Reports:
  Responses from the Educational Com-
  munity," 44

Tarule, J., 13
Teacher (Ashton-Warner), 103, 111, 113–
  115
Teacher education and teacher educators
  Haley on, 109
  sanitized images of teaching promoted
    by, 3
Teachers and teaching
  bread baking metaphor of, 23
  class backgrounds of, 31
  complexities of, 6, 15, 21, 63
  confidence of, 84
  confronting silence of, 12–14
  as craft, 1, 3
  criticisms of, 10, 31–32
  despair of, 69
  dilemmas of, 83

  efficiency of, 27–28
  empowerment of, 32, 95, 110
  feeling conflicted in, 84
  feminization of, 87
  fly-fishing metaphor of, 2
  gardening metaphor of, 23
  genders of, 87–88
  history of, 100, 122
  hopes and intentionality of, 7
  indirect study of, 15–16
  isolation of, 26–27, 69, 91, 95
  messiness of, 21, 28, 37
  moods of, 29–30
  moral dimensions of, 6, 9
  physical appearances of, 48–49
  place of provision in, 64–65
  practical wisdom of, 8
  predictability of, 3, 7–8, 37
  professionalization of, 102, 106–107,
    122–123
  races of, 95
  as rational activity, 60
  relations of, 1–2, 13–14, 22, 49–50,
    54–55, 101, 115, 118–119, 122,
    125*n*
  revaluation of, 68
  reversing emphasis of, 18
  ringmaster metaphor of, 35
  studies of intersection of life cycle and,
    96
  teacher mediated access to, 16
  technical conceptions of, 9
  vulnerability of, 32, 55–56
"Teachers' Stories as Research and Reflection" (Walizer), 128*n*
Team teaching, 80
Tempest, The (Shakespeare), 34–36
Tenderness, hostility and, 21–22
Tests and testing, 31–32
  of intelligence, 109
  teacher empowerment and, 32
Textmaking in reading teaching, 17
Textual criticism, 15–16, 125*n*–126*n*
  benefits of, 35
Thanksgiving, writing assignments on,
  52–53
Thomas, Donald W., 56–64, 66–67
Thoreau, Henry David, 117
Thoughtfulness, pressures to avoid, 99
"Torpedo's Touch, The" (Thomas), 56

Toughness, affection and, 51
Town meetings, 84
Tracking
    Coalition of Essential Schools in target-
        ing of, 99
    racial polarization in, 86
Transformative teaching, mimetic teaching
    vs., 64
Tropes, 97, 111
Tutoring, 39–41
Twain, Mark, 110–111
Two-eyed reading, 14

Uncertainty and uncertainties
    acceptance of, 7
    acknowledgment of, 7
    coping with, 41
    genuine questioning as result of facing,
        41
    of life, 7
    mindfulness of, 100
    negotiation of, 90
    in professional judgment, 84, 86
    repression of, 2
    tolerance of, 100, 111
Unions and unionism
    contracts negotiated by, 73
    Haley on, 102, 105–109
Urban schools, suburban teachers in, 49

Velcro essays, 25–27
    grading of, 26–27
Vocational education, Haley on, 109

Walden (Thoreau), 117
Walizer, Marue, 128*n*
Waller, W., 83–84

Wehmiller, P. L., 23
Wheeler, C. W., 38
Wheelock College, 127*n*
White Teacher (Paley), 113
Whitman, Walt, 110–111
Wigginton, Eliot, 17, 101–105, 107, 111,
    115–122, 128*n*
    accomplishments of, 103
    in applying cold standards to students,
        120
    commitment of, 104
    on holding oneself accountable, 102–
        104, 117, 119–120
    log home of, 115–116
    teaching background of, 116–117
    teaching stories of, 118–120
Wise, A., 5
Wittrock, M. C., 125*n*
Women's Ways of Knowing (Belenky,
        Clinchy, Goldberger, & Tarule), 13
Work, meaning of, 51
World War I, Haley's opposition to, 108
Writing and writing assignments. *See also*
        Journal writing
    autobiographical, 25–27
    conflicts over, 54–55
    on families on Thanksgiving, 52–53
    integrating reading and, 52
    skill levels of students contrasted in,
        85–86
    storytelling and differences between
        reading and, 71

Yin, R. K., 127*n*
Young, Ella Flagg, 107

Zajac, Chris, 7–8, 17

About the Author

The author was a high school teacher for 17 years, and now works with high school teachers in the Coalition of Essential Schools, where he is a senior researcher. He holds a teaching appointment in education at Brown University, where he has taught graduate and undergraduate students. The research reported in this book was completed while the author was a Spencer Fellow of the National Academy of Education.